Physical Fitness and the Older Person

A Guide to Exercise for Health Care Professionals

Contributors

M. Neel Buell

Thomas K. Cureton

Maryellen Kelleher

Carole Lewis

Susan L. Sandel

Robert E. Wear

Physical Fitness and the Older Person

A Guide to Exercise for Health Care Professionals

Editor
Leonard Biegel

AN ASPEN PUBLICATION®
Aspen Systems Corporation
Rockville, Maryland
Royal Tunbridge Wells
1984

Library of Congress Cataloging in Publication Data
Main entry under title:

Physical fitness and the older person.

"An Aspen publication."
Includes bibliographical references and index.
1. Exercise for the aged. 2. Physical fitness for the aged. 3. Exercise
therapy. I. Biegel, Leonard. [DNLM: 1. Exertion — in old age.
2. Physical Fitness. QT 255 P5785]
RA781.P565   1984   613.7'1   84-6328
ISBN: 0-89443-894-8

Publisher: John R. Marozsan
Associate Publisher: Jack W. Knowles, Jr.
Editorial Director: Margaret M. Quinlin
Executive Managing Editor: Margot G. Raphael
Managing Editor: M. Eileen Higgins
Editorial Services: Scott Ballotin
Printing and Manufacturing: Debbie Collins

Library of Congress Catalog Card Number: 84-6328
ISBN: 0-89443-894-8

Printed in the United States of America

1   2   3   4   5

To Uncle Sidney

Table of Contents

Preface xi

Chapter 1—Fitness: Who, What, and Why 1
    Leonard Biegel

    Adult Fitness Trends 1
    Older Adults' Perceptions of Fitness Programs ... 3
    Understanding the Fitness Needs of
        Older Adults 4
    Research-Supported Advantages of Fitness
        for Older Adults 4
    Fitness and Self-Image 7
    Improving Adult Fitness 7
    The Delaying Effects of Exercise on the
        Aging Process 8
    The Declining Adult Mortality Rate 9
    Conclusion 11

Chapter 2—Sex, Attitudes, Aging Processes, and
           Exercise Guidelines 13
    Leonard Biegel

    Changing Attitudes toward Female
        Sports Participants 13
    Physical Characteristics Color Attitudes toward
        Sports Participants 14
    Growth Traits of Children 14

Physiological Response of Women to
Exercise 16
Maintaining Proper Body Function
through Exercise 18
Exercise Guidelines for the Older Adult 19
Rating the Fitness Programs 22
Devices That Don't Develop Fitness 25

**Chapter 3—Psychosocial Advantages of Fitness Programs
for Older People 27**
M. Neel Buell

Personal Testimonies—Participating in
Fitness Programs 27
Common Myths about Exercising 28
Physiological Benefits of Exercise 30
Personal Testimonies—Exercise Restores the
Aging Body 30
Psychosocial Benefits of Fitness 31

Chapter 4—Rating the Programs 41
Thomas K. Cureton

Introduction 41
Definition of Terms 42
Physiological Benefits of Exercise 42
Rating the Programs 43
Conclusions 49

Chapter 5—Getting Started and Monitoring Progress 51
Leonard Biegel

Exercising in Groups 51
Organizing the Group 52
Pre-Exercise Fitness Evaluation 53
The First Meeting 56
Lifestyle Inventory 56
Designing the Exercise Program 57
Analyzing Results 58

Chapter 6—Calisthenics for Active Older Individuals **61**
Robert E. Wear

Introduction 61
Goals 61
General Guidelines 62
Incorporating Exercise into Everyday Activity ... 64
Additional Notes of Caution and Precaution 64
Specific Programs 65

**Chapter 7—Walking: Oft Neglected, Highly
　　　　　Recommended** **89**
Leonard Biegel

Walking As Aerobic Exercise 89
Walking As a Prescription for Fitness 90
Characteristics of a Walking Program 91
Ground Rules 93

Chapter 8—Dance/Movement Therapy **101**
Susan L. Sandel and Maryellen Kelleher

Inactivity and Aging 101
Treatment Modalities 102
Conclusion 116

Chapter 9—In the Swim **119**
Leonard Biegel

Introduction 119
Swimming Program Attributes 119
Cautionary Notes 120
Exercises for Swimming 121

Chapter 10—Arthritis and Exercise **129**
Carole Lewis

What is Arthritis? 129
Osteoarthritis 129
Rheumatoid Arthritis 130
Polymyalgia Rheumatica 130

Exercise As an Intervention Program
    for Arthritis 131
Conclusions 149

Chapter 11—Food for Fitness **151**
    Leonard Biegel

Nutritional Requirements of Older Adults 151
Nutritional Requirements of Young
    vs. Old Adults 152
Presenting Dietary Information 154
Obesity and Other Dietary Health Risks 155
Caloric Intake and Expenditure 155

Index **157**

Preface

The past several years have witnessed a striking change in the awareness of the benefits of—and the consequences of disregarding—physical fitness. During this time, America's older population has made considerable strides in addressing its particular fitness concerns. People over 65, particularly if they are retired and not severely restricted in their movements, have the time and capacity to participate in fitness programs. Indeed, as a recent report, *Aging in the Eighties,* notes, 25 percent of the respondents over 65 are walking, jogging or otherwise exercising in significant amounts.*

The remaining 75 percent of older Americans is clearly a population in need of fitness programs. For, as the evidence in the following chapters documents, exercise improves not only the quality of life but longevity prospects as well.

Fitness programs can take a variety of forms, from walking alone to calisthenics in a group. Choosing, organizing, and starting on a program are often the challenging first steps toward fitness. The results, numerous testimonies report, are worth the effort.

Leonard Biegel

---

*Louis Harris, *Aging in the Eighties: America in Transition* (Washington, D.C.: National Council on the Aging).

Chapter 1

Fitness: Who, What, and Why

Leonard Biegel

Exercise has become an adult fashion in America. Tennis, running, squash, racquetball, swimming, and other pursuits are practiced so widely they are now big business. Entire stores are devoted to adult fitness clothing and equipment. Countless runners wearing designer labels fill city streets and country paths daily.

ADULT FITNESS TRENDS

While no definitive study indicates how many people benefit from properly performed exercise, a number of surveys are worth examining for trends.

The U.S. National Center for Health Statistics' most recent figures, compiled in 1975, reported that over 42 percent of adults ages 45 and over exercise regularly (see Table 1–1).

According to the *Perrier Study of Fitness in America* approximately 60 percent of adult Americans claim that they exercise regularly. Of that 60 percent, 15 percent report 5 hours a week of vigorous physical activity; 16 percent report 3½ to 5 hours; and 28 percent, 2½ to 3½ hours.[1]

The same survey, looking at adults 18 and older, delineated the most popular fitness activities:

Table 1–1 Percent of Adults Exercising Regularly, by Age and Type of Exercise Performed

Age	Total Population (×1,000)	Percent Exercising Regularly*	Bicycling (%)	Calisthenics (%)	Jogging (%)	Weight Lifting (%)	Swimming (%)	Walking (%)	All Other Exercise (%)
Total, 20 years and over	135,655	48.6	10.9	13.5	4.8	3.4	11.8	33.8	6.8
20–44 years	71,084	53.7	16.1	17.3	7.3	5.4	16.9	33.8	6.9
45–64 years	43,145	43.4	6.5	10.8	2.7	1.5	8.0	32.9	6.5
65 years and older	21,426	42.3	2.9	6.1	1.2	8	2.8	35.7	6.9

*Regular exercise was defined as any exercise performed on at least a weekly basis. Persons responding were permitted to report more than one exercise.

Source: Adapted from U.S. National Center for Health Statistics, *Health, United States, 1976-1977,* Department of Health, Education and Welfare Publication No. (HRA) 77–1232, p. 202.

Walking	— 22%	Tennis	— 9%
Swimming	— 17%	Basketball	— 7%
Calisthenics	— 14%	Hiking	— 7%
Bicycling	— 13%	Softball	— 7%
Running	— 11%	Baseball	— 6%

The Correlation between Income and Exercise Levels

A 1978 Harris survey found that affluent people are more likely than lower income people to engage in regular exercise.[2] Whether the reasons are more leisure time, the ability to pay for related expenses (program or membership fees, equipment and clothing, etc.) or the general correlation with higher income and education, the figures are important. Only 24 percent of adults in households with an income of less than $7,000 a year reported obtaining regular exercise. The percentage rose to 56 percent in households earning $25,000 a year or more; among business leaders, it was a startling 75 percent.

In considering survey data about exercise levels, it should be understood that the figures are generally understated, for they do not include exercise obtained while on the job or from doing household chores. Twenty-four percent of men, but only 10 percent of women, report a great deal of physical activity at work. Another 26 percent of men and 18 percent of women report some job-related physical activity.[3]

OLDER ADULTS' PERCEPTIONS OF FITNESS PROGRAMS

Casey Conrad, executive director of the President's Council on Physical Fitness and Sports, makes the following comments on older people's perceptions of fitness programs:

- They believe their need for exercise diminishes and eventually disappears as they grow older.
- They vastly exaggerate the risks involved in vigorous exercise after middle age.

- They overrate the benefits of light, sporadic exercise.
- They underrate their own abilities and capacities.[4]

UNDERSTANDING THE FITNESS NEEDS OF OLDER ADULTS

The purpose of this book is to help gerontology professionals understand the physical fitness needs of older adults; to clarify the advantages and options in specific programs; to provide professionals enough background to match older adults with the program that will benefit them most; and to assist in implementing the programs. At the outset, it is important to understand the nature of physical fitness.

In its more general terms, physical fitness is the ability to carry out daily tasks with vigor and alertness, without undue fatigue, and with ample energy to enjoy leisure-time pursuits and to meet unusual situations and unforeseen emergencies. The definition implies that physical fitness is more than "not being sick" or merely "being well."

RESEARCH-SUPPORTED ADVANTAGES OF FITNESS FOR OLDER ADULTS

According to various studies, including the *Physical Fitness Research Digest,* published by the President's Council on Physical Fitness and Sports in April 1977,[5] the research-supported advantages of exercise for older people include:

- *Mental Achievement.* Most studies demonstrated a positive relationship between physical-motor traits and mental achievement. A person's *general learning potential for a given level of intelligence* increases or decreases in accordance with the degree of physical fitness.

- *Personal-Social Status.* Positive relationships exist between physical-motor traits and personal-social characteristics, peer status indicators, and self-concept instruments.

- *Minimizing Tensions and Raising Morale.* Herbert deVries and Gene Adams, physiologists, contrasted the tranquilizing effect of exercise upon ten tense ("anxious") men and women between 52 and 70 years of age. Muscular tension was measured by electromyography, using surface electrodes. The results showed that 15 minutes of walking at a heart rate of 100 beats per minute lowered electrical activity in the musculature 20 percent. Neither meprobamate nor placebo treatments had a significantly more relaxing effect. Thus, in single doses, at least, exercise had as much effect upon reducing tension, and without any undesirable side effects, as did the tranquilizer drug.[6]

- *Minimizing Coronary Heart Disease.* An overwhelming majority of studies on adults from several countries supports an inverse relationship between the amount of daily physical activity and the incidence of coronary heart disease. Regular physical activity does not invariably prevent a heart attack but does make its occurrence much less likely; furthermore, in the event of an attack, it tends to be less severe and the likelihood of survival is greater among the physically fit. Utilizing cardiopulmonary endurance regimens of exercise, with appropriate intensity and dosage continued regularly over a period of time, the following results have been achieved with adults: reduction in serum cholesterol and triglyceride levels; development of collateral circulation around coronary artery restrictions; improvement in myocardial vascularization; increase in red blood cells and blood volume; improved fibrinolytic capability; and reduction in blood pressure. Mild exercise also appears to aid in the destruction of blood clots. One study concluded that 10 weeks of exercise sharply increased the participants' production of a protein that dissolves a clotting agent.

- *Minimizing Peripheral Vascular Disease.* As reported by Nathan Pritikin et al.,[7] the Longevity Research Institute of Santa Barbara and the Veterans Administration Hospital of Long Beach, California, studied the treatment of peripheral vascular disease through diet modification and walking over a six-month period (80 percent of the patients in the study had previously undergone arterial reconstruction surgery). Nineteen patients were assigned to each of two groups. Both groups walked daily as much as they could. The experimental factor was the diet: the control group consumed the conventional diet for cardiac patients (20 percent protein, 40 percent fat, 40 percent carbohydrates, and 300 mg cholesterol daily). The diet for the experimental group contained 10 percent protein, 10 percent fat, 80 percent carbohydrates (simple and unrefined), and no cholesterol. On a treadmill walking test, the control group improved 302 percent; the experimental group's improvement was 5,802 percent! Coexisting diseases in the experimental group (but not in the control group) improved in the following percentages: 100 percent of patients with angina, diabetes previously treated with oral hypoglycemics, gout, arthritis, and elevated blood lipids; 75 percent of those with hypertension and diet-controlled diabetes; and 50 percent (or more) of insulin-dependent diabetics and congestive heart failure patients. Arterial plaque reduction also occurred to some degree.

- *Minimizing Other Organic Conditions*. Hans Kraus and Wilhelm Raab developed the concept of "hypokinetic disease," defined as the "whole spectrum of inactivity-induced somatic and mental derangement."[8] In addition to coronary heart disease, they indicated that other internal diseases, including diabetes and ulcers, are more frequent in the sedentary than in the active. Eighty percent of low back pain, they insist, is due to lack of adequate physical activity; lack of physical exercise also parallels emotional difficulties; and the physically active show better adaptability to stress, less neuromuscular tension, and less tendency toward fatigue. Active persons age later, do not tend toward obesity, have lower blood pressure, are stronger and more flexible, and have greater breathing capacity.

- *Fat Reduction*. Jean Mayer, a nutritionist at Harvard University, contends that physical inactivity is the single most important factor explaining the increasing frequency of overweight people in modern western societies. Intensive physical conditioning causes a depletion of excess fat and an increase in lean body weight. Whether or not there is an appreciable change in body weight, body composition changes, with a decrease in body fat and a corresponding increase in muscular tissue.[9]

FITNESS AND SELF-IMAGE

According to a survey conducted by Research and Forecast, Inc., for Americana Health Care Corporation in 1980, perception of good health is the strongest influence on an older person's feeling of optimism.[10] In the study, half of the elderly individuals reported their health to be good to excellent. These individuals reported that they are not depressed; have strong self-images; have a high sense of the worth of things; feel useful and secure; do not experience tension, restlessness or confusion; and never have trouble thinking clearly. Members of the other half reported fair to poor health and, consequently, had poor self-images.

IMPROVING ADULT FITNESS

Thomas K. Cureton, director of the Physical Fitness Institute at the University of Illinois, and author of Chapter 4 in this book, is a world-famed investigator and practitioner of ways by which adult physical fitness can be improved and sustained. For over a quarter century, he has conducted and sponsored numerous studies (using his graduate students as test subjects) on exercise regimens for adults.

Cureton has summarized much of this work. One report, which is an evaluation of 20 types of fitness programs, including his continuous, rhythmical endurance process, jogging, the Canadian 5BX program, swimming, calisthenics, weight training, isometrics, and various other sports, concluded that progressive rhythmic types of exercise are beneficial in obtaining circulatory system improvements in adults. The amount of time devoted to exercising emerged as an important factor: programs of five to six days a week were superior to programs of one, two, and three days per week; also, regimens of one hour per day were better than one-half hour or less.[11]

THE DELAYING EFFECTS OF EXERCISE ON THE AGING PROCESS

Cureton documents the physiological effects of exercise on adults by citing 200 studies. Among the most significant conclusions are the following:

- Men—even young men—are not doing enough vigorous exercise to keep the blood flowing rapidly through the muscles in adequate amounts, an important key to physical fitness. Thus, physiological aging comes upon modern man with astonishing rapidity, especially for those who are sedentary.
- In the trained (or fit) state, the nervous system is prepared for action rather than inaction. In general, one can be trained away from persistent sedentary tendencies and toward a high sympathetic and vagus tone leading toward a desire for physical activity.
- Strength per pound of body weight increases as a result of force and speed power exercises. Strength is vital to move the body about continuously in walking, running, swimming, climbing, hiking with a pack, bicycling uphill, and in daily activities.
- Health, endurance, nutrition, and a sense of well-being are dependent upon a common denominator—circulatory fitness. The one way to gain and maintain this fitness is through systematic exercise that requires adjustment of the cardiopulmonary system to the activity.
- Bodily movement trains the heart and improves circulation. In movement, stimulation of the sympathetic branches of the autonomic nervous system occurs. Lack of movement leads to deterioration of the circulation, as will happen, for example, with enforced bed rest.
- The heart is not a vacuum pump and cannot suck the blood up from the feet and legs to the heart when the body is upright. Muscular movements, involuntary contractions, and wave pulsation force blood to return to the heart. The use of the legs in exercise significantly expedites the efficient return flow of blood

to the heart, a sound reason for including leg exercises, jogging or walking, and swimming in the physical fitness program.

- Exercise dilates capillaries. The muscles, heart, spinal cord, brain, lungs, and nerves (all the organs) are permeated by countless numbers of capillaries. These tiny vessels are controlled by microscopic nerves. Exercise stimulates the nerves and causes them to produce capillary dilation. Thus, the capillaries are not fixed in size; some may be very narrow but able to expand according to need. Exercise is necessary for their optimum effectiveness.[12]

THE DECLINING ADULT MORTALITY RATE

Everywhere one turns, there is news of the "graying of America." The trend is irreversible, as our birth rate has declined and people are living longer. How much longer? The following life expectancies have been charted by the U.S. National Center for Health Statistics (see Table 1–2):

Table 1–2 Life Expectancy of Americans Aged 65 and over (in Years)

Current Age	Average for All Groups	White		Black and Other	
		Male	Female	Male	Female
65	16.6	14.2	18.7	13.3	17.2
70	13.4	11.3	15.0	10.7	13.9
75	10.6	8.8	11.7	8.6	11.5
80	8.4	6.9	9.0	7.8	10.7
85 and over	6.7	5.5	7.0	6.8	9.2

Source: Adapted from the U.S. National Center for Health Statistics, *Vital Statistics of the United States, 1979;* and *Statistical Abstract of the United States, National Data Book and Guide to Sources,* 103rd ed., 1982–1983, Washington, D.C.: Health Resources Administration, © 1983, p. 72.

Throughout the industrial world, improvements in sanitation, nutrition, housing, and education have contributed to a significant decline in the death rate since 1900. While the leading causes of death in 1900 were infectious diseases—particularly pneumonia and tuberculosis—the causes today are quite different—heart disease tops the list, followed by cancer, stroke, and accidents.

Coronary artery disease is the leading cause of death in the United States. It is responsible for 640,000 deaths each year, including almost one-third of all deaths of 35 to 64 year olds. On the average, almost three Americans suffer a heart attack every minute of every day, a total of approximately one and a half million each year.

The Decline between 1950 and 1977

Between 1950 and 1970, the U.S. mortality rate from heart disease decreased. For white men and women, the rate dropped 9 percent and 25 percent, respectively. For black men and women, the rate fell 28 percent and 10 percent. Through 1977, the rates of decline became more equal—18 percent and 19 percent for white and black women and 15 percent and 14 percent for white and black men.[13]

A number of factors suggest explanations for the decline in heart disease mortality:

- decreased smoking
- improved management of hypertension
- decreased dietary intake of saturated fats
- improved medical emergency services
- more widespread use and increased efficiency of coronary care units
- more widespread physical activity.

In part, the same factors apply to a decline in death due to stroke (particularly, management of hypertension). Thus, prevention, not cure, has become an increasingly vital factor in longevity.

The Link between Exercise and Longer Life

According to the President's Council on Physical Fitness and Sports, the conclusions of a ten-year study (beginning in 1965 and tracking 7,000 subjects) were that regular exercise, in combination with other good living habits, can help increase life expectancy by as much as 11 years for men and 7 years for women.[14] Twice as many deaths occurred among the men who exercised infrequently as there were among those who exercised regularly. One of the physicians who wrote the study report declared that "the daily habits of people have a great deal more to do with what makes them sick and when they die than do the influences of medicine."[15]

The U.S. Public Health Service remains cautious, stating that no conclusive data exist that clearly establish the effects of exercise and physical fitness on reducing risks of disease. Yet, according to the health service, "sedentary living has been established as one of the factors that increase the probabilities of cardiovascular disease."[16]

CONCLUSION

The value of regular physical activity is clear, and participation should be a goal of all Americans. Public recreation departments and private agencies that sponsor physical activity programs should encourage the development of physical fitness and sports skills for all age groups. In addition, health professionals should guide their patients toward participation in appropriate exercise regimens.

NOTES

1. Perrier Study of Fitness in America.

2. Louis Harris, *Aging in the Eighties: America in Transition* (Washington, D.C.: National Council on the Aging).

3. Ibid.

4. President's Council on Physical Fitness and Sports, *Physical Fitness Research Digest* 7(2) (April 1977): 1–2.

5. Ibid., p. 3.

6. Herbert A. deVries and Gene M. Adams, "Electromyographic Comparison of Single Doses of Exercise and Meprobamate as to Effects on Muscular Relaxation," *American Journal of Physical Medicine* 51 (1972): 130.

7. Nathan Pritikin et al., *Diet and Exercise As a Total Therapeutic Regimen for Rehabilitation of Patients with Severe Peripheral Vascular Disease*, paper presented before the American Congress of Rehabilitation Medicine, Nov. 19, 1975.

8. Hans Kraus and Wilhelm Raab, *Hypokinetic Disease* (Springfield, Ill.: Charles C Thomas, 1964).

9. Jean Mayer, *Overweight: Causes, Cost and Control* (Englewood Cliffs, N.J.: Prentice-Hall, 1968).

10. Research and Forecast, Inc., Americana Health Care Corporation, 1980.

11. Thomas K. Cureton, "Adult Fitness Improvements," *Journal of Physical Education* (March-April 1974): 112.

12. Thomas K. Cureton, *The Physiological Effects of Exercise Programs on Adults* (Springfield, Ill.: Charles C Thomas, 1969), pp. 15–22.

13. National Center for Health Statistics, *Vital Statistics of the United States, 1979* (Washington, D.C.: Health Resources Administration, 1979).

14. The President's Council on Physical Fitness and Sports (Washington, D.C.: U.S. Department of Health, Education, and Welfare, Publication No. OS-77-50013, 1978).

15. Ibid.

16. Ibid.

Chapter 2

Sex, Attitudes, Aging Processes, and Exercise Guidelines

Leonard Biegel

More evidence is now available (perhaps as a result of the women's movement) to answer some of the age-old questions about men's and women's differing physical abilities. Some of the differences may be cultural; others may have a biological basis.

CHANGING ATTITUDES TOWARD FEMALE SPORTS PARTICIPANTS

The very language of sport has tended to make the female an intruder in a segregated place. Thus, if a boy "plays like a man," how does a girl play? If a tough scrimmage for males "separates the men from the boys," what does such a scrimmage do for females? If a vigorous, soiled, shirt-tailed boy is "all boy," what is a girl with these qualities? If the terms "athletic" and "athletic build" suggest an admirable male, what do they suggest when applied to a female?[1]

Because the need for sex role differentiation has begun to vanish, females as well as males are now freer to pursue their individual interests rather than conform to a role stereotype. Thus, the female athlete is less likely to be perceived as trying to act like a man than simply as a human being at play.

While much of the gathering evidence on active sports participation has concentrated on the young, a rippling attitudinal effect is reaching the older population. Whether through the mass media or through contact with relatives and friends, women of all ages are expressing serious concern about their hitherto frail image.

PHYSICAL CHARACTERISTICS COLOR ATTITUDES TOWARD SPORTS PARTICIPANTS

According to Dorothy Harris, writing in *Women in Sports,* it is important to take into account some general male and female characteristics that color attitudes toward sports in the early years. She indicated that almost all sports discriminate against those who are weaker, slower, and less powerful, regardless of whether they are male or female. Since males on the average are stronger, faster and more powerful than females, they have inherent advantages in sports requiring these attributes. This advantage becomes most dramatic with the onset of adolescence and the maturation of the endocrine system, which influences physical stature, musculature, and strength. Thus, biology is the starting point for any discussion of sex differences.[2]

Biologically, Harris states, the degree of physical difference observed between the sexes may be explained by the difference in each sex's characteristic ratio of androgens to estrogens.[3] The greatest physical differences between the sexes occur from puberty onward through the active reproductive years, when sex hormones are at their greatest levels. During this period, males have higher levels of androgens, which promote greater muscle mass, larger and denser bones, and increased strength. Females have higher levels of estrogens, which shorten their growing period and increase accumulation of fat tissue. While some females are capable of performing sports activities at higher levels than some males, the percentage who can do so is small. In general, therefore, competing for positions on the same sports teams will discriminate against females.

GROWTH TRAITS OF CHILDREN

Some of the growth traits of children are important not only as characteristics of males and females but as early influences on the ability to participate in fitness programs. The older persons' early experiences affect their attitudes and/or perceptions of exercise.

- *Height.* The gain in height is consistent for most boys from age 6 to 13. For the average girl, this gain is also consistent until age 11. The difference in height between the sexes is quite small until the start of girls' adolescent period. At age 11, girls surge ahead of boys in height as they reach adolescence earlier. Within a few years, however, boys' adolescent growth spurt begins to establish the adult male superiority in height.
- *Weight.* Weight gain also occurs in a similar pattern in both sexes.
- *Shoulder-Hip Differences.* The differences between males and females in shoulder and hip width become apparent at adolescence. In shoulder width, boys follow the usual growth pattern, having a much greater spurt than girls do; in hip width, the opposite occurs. Generally, then, girls aged 12 to 13 years have narrower shoulders and broader hips than do boys.
- *Leg-Trunk Proportion.* In the preadolescent years, differences in mean leg lengths of same-age boys and girls are not significant. Yet, in adults the leg lengths of males relative to trunk length are greater than for females. During adolescence, the major gain in height is due to growth of the legs, not to lengthening of the trunk.
- *Arm Length.* The arms of boys are consistently longer than the arms of girls, largely because of longer forearms. Unlike most other sex-related physical differences, disparity in arm length does not occur primarily during adolescence, but is already established at age two (and continues to grow greater till adolescence).
- *Adipose (Fatty) Tissue.* Girls have somewhat more adipose tissue than do boys, especially from ages five or six onward. From ages one to six, girls lose fat more slowly than boys, and they gain fat more rapidly after age six. At adolescence, some acceleration in female fat gain starts shortly before, and continues until after, the main adolescent growth spurt. For girls, from age six onward, adipose tissue increases steadily throughout the growth period.

- *Musculature*. In early childhood, boys have slightly more muscle than girls do, although the sex differences remain slight until the adolescent growth spurt. At adolescence, a large skeletal muscle increase occurs in boys, coinciding roughly with increases in height and weight. For girls, muscle gains during this period are not nearly so great.
- *Skeletal System*. At birth, the bones of the skeleton are not completely calcified; some are still entirely cartilaginous. Ossification of the skeletal system is not complete until maturity. At birth, girls are generally ahead in skeletal development by a few weeks; the gap increases until it has reached a margin of about two years at adolescence.
- *Heart Size*. The heart muscle begins rapid growth about one year before the sudden growth in height, and is well established before puberty. The heart muscle growth spurt occurs in both sexes but is more marked in boys.
- *Heart Rate*. The heart rate falls gradually from birth through maturity. The average rate of decline is about the same for boys and girls until age 11; thereafter, the boys' rate decreases more rapidly. In adults, the heart rate is approximately 10 percent greater in women than in men.[4]
- *Metabolism*. The basal metabolic rate falls constantly from birth onward, not only to maturity but extending into old age. There are slight checks in this downward trend between ages 12 and 13 (for boys) and about two years earlier for girls. At all ages, boys' metabolic rates are greater than girls', relative to body surface area. This sex difference is due partially to the male mesomorphic and the female endomorphic tendencies, demonstrating that muscle has a greater resting oxygen consumption rate than does fat.[5]

PHYSIOLOGICAL RESPONSES OF WOMEN TO EXERCISE

Barbara Drinkwater, writing in *Exercise and Sports Sciences Review,* presented an extensive review of the physiological responses of women to exercise. She questioned whether or not a female response to exercise exists that is due solely to the factor of sex.[6] While the maximum aerobic capacity of the average woman is less than that of the average man, differences are influenced by factors other than sex.

1. A person's level of physical fitness overrides the factor of sex. In studies utilizing skiing, swimming, and track, young female athletes had maximum aerobic capacities equal to or better than those of nonathletic, same-age males.

2. Even among nonathletes, considerable variability in aerobic capacity exists within the sexes and thus the broad spectrum of maximum aerobic values cannot be dichotomized on the basis of sex.

3. However, when a male athlete is compared to a female athlete, the male has a decided advantage. On the average, he will exceed the woman's maximal oxygen intake by 20 percent to 25 percent (compared to a 10 percent to 20 percent differential found between mean values in normal populations).*

4. For equal submaximal loads, women usually work at a higher percentage of their maximal aerobic capacity than do men.

In general, however, information on women's physiological response to exercise is relatively meager (in comparison to that available for men). Still, enough contradictions are already apparent in the literature to make it difficult, if not impossible, to generalize about the female's response to physical activity. Two major problems in determining if there is a sex-mediated response are (1) the lack of a standard method for presenting data and (2) the variation in experimental design between studies. This information lag will close as the physical fitness movement continues.

---

*Some investigators have reported that this difference disappears when maximal intake is expressed in relation to fat-free body weight or active muscle mass. The conflicting results among the studies may be related to the use of different methods for calculating fat-free weight and to differences in relative physical fitness between male and female subjects.

MAINTAINING PROPER BODY FUNCTION THROUGH EXERCISE

Efficiency and Endurance of the Heart and Lungs

Proper functioning of the heart, lungs, and blood vessels is probably the most important aspect of fitness in the adult years. Vital to fitness is a strong and responsive heart that can pump the blood needed to nourish billions of body cells, unimpaired lung capacity for the efficient exchange of cell metabolism byproducts with lifegiving oxygen, and elastic, unobstructed blood vessels.

Activities involving the leg muscles help maintain good circulation by the "squeezing" action of the muscles on the veins; this benefit cannot be achieved in any other way. Scientific research evidence increasingly points to the importance of regular physical activity in maintaining efficient cardiopulmonary function.

Muscular Strength and Endurance

Muscles grow in size and strength only if used; otherwise they become soft and flabby and lose strength and elasticity. Although strength does decrease with age, the rate of decline can be retarded through regular exercise that keeps the muscles toned.

Balance

Proper function of the balance mechanism is extremely important in the fitness of older people and is maintained through performance of daily activities. Some elderly individuals tend to lose their sense of balance much more quickly than others the same age. The problem is compounded by the need to use bi-focal or tri-focal glasses. A well-maintained sense of balance can help compensate for potential hazards caused by quick changes in vision when going from one optical focus to another.

Flexibility

The aging process—aggravated by disuse—causes the tissues surrounding the joints to thicken and lose elasticity. Moving the joints in a proper exercise program can delay this process. Exercise also helps forestall the onset of arthritis, one of the most common and painful diseases associated with old age. Exercise that stretches the muscles can help keep them supple (and prevent shortening and tightening).

Our traditional concern for older people is a mixed blessing. We put push buttons within easy reach and keep shelving low, thus avoiding the necessity for bending and stretching. Older people should be encouraged to move through a wide range of motion in order to keep joints flexible, muscles supple, and the heart pumping at maximum efficiency.

Coordination and Agility

A well-coordinated individual can direct body parts in skillful movement, coordinate different actions, and move and change directions quickly and safely.

Professional-calibre athletic skills are not essential in later years. But for the enjoyment of recreation and the safe performance of daily activities, one should exercise regularly in order to maintain reasonably good levels of coordination and agility.

EXERCISE GUIDELINES FOR THE OLDER ADULT

Evidence indicates that older adults can improve fitness through appropriate exercise programs (see Chapters 3 and 4). Before analyzing specific fitness program choices, it is important to note some general guidelines:

- *Exercise should be adapted to the individual's tolerance.* Exercise tolerance refers to the individual's ability to perform a given exercise, a series of exercises, or activities involving exercise at a specified dosage without undue discomfort or fatigue. An exercise regimen that is too easy deprives the individual of the full benefits of exercise; on the other hand, exercise that is difficult (or impossible) to perform can be dangerous (because of overexertion) or, at the least, frustrating.

- *The exercise plan should provide for progression.* The exercise plan should start with an understanding of the individual's current exercise tolerance; then, within this tolerance level, it should provide for moderate overloading of the muscles to develop strength and increase the demands on the cardio-respiratory system (to improve endurance). Progression should be applied by gradually increasing exercise in a logical way, thus keeping demands just ahead of improvement. Progression may be accompanied by increasing the intensity or duration of exercise, or both.

- *Psychological as well as physiological limits must be attained.* For persons unaccustomed to strenuous physical exertion, psychological tolerance for exercise may be reached well before physiological limits are attained. Psychological limits may be conditioned by habit, slight aches, breathlessness, and by such mental factors as anxiety, boredom, and fear of physical injury. Such mildly distressful feelings halt exercise before appreciable overloading has occurred; consequently, only minimal increases in strength and endurance result. (Careful judgment must be used by the exercise instructor, since certain psychological limits also serve as safeguards against overstrain.) A progressive approach to exercise dosage should resolve this problem, as the individual gradually learns to accept strenuous exercise and to realize his or her true limits.

- *Individuals must desire to improve.* Motivation to become (and stay) fit is essential if an individual is to adopt exercise as a way of life. A knowledge of the benefits of exercise can provide this motivation.

- *A thorough consultation with a physician should precede a fitness program.* Sedentary older persons, in particular, should check against any abnormalities of the cardiovascular and respiratory systems before embarking on a vigorous exercise regimen. Stress testing may also be desirable, especially for those with symptoms or histories of cardiovascular abnormalities or with family histories of coronary problems. The sedentary individual should approach exercise gradually and determine tolerance by feelings of fatigue or distress, confirmed by objective documentation from stress testing. While one of the primary goals of exercise is to strengthen the heart muscle, it is important to know the condition of the heart before exercising begins. Many physicians recommend a stress electrocardiogram (in addition to a resting electrocardiogram). Stress electrocardiograms are gaining popularity (1) because of their tendency to uncover subtle abnormalities that may lead to heart attack, and (2) because they provide a rational basis for determining what can be done to improve heart musculature that shows evidence of damage.

- *Warming up is an essential part of any exercise program.* The body must be prepared for vigorous activity by "warming up." Any individual, especially an older person, should avoid sudden initiation of strenuous activity. The warm-up period should begin with continuous rhythmical activity (such as walking), gradually increasing the intensity until pulse rate, breathing, and body temperature are elevated slightly. It is also desirable to do some easy stretching, pulling, and rotating exercises during the warm-up period. Specific warm-up exercises are included in Chapter 6.

- *Alternating periods of vigorous activity with periods of lesser stress.* By gradually increasing the proportion of stressful to less stressful exercise in the workout, physical condition will improve. This principle—called "interval training"—can be applied to many forms of exercise and is particularly adaptable to walking, jogging, and swimming.

- *Using the overload principle.* The correct way to structure an exercise program is to use the "overload principle"—that is, gradually increase exercise intensity (or repetitions) in successive workouts, challenging the body to work a little harder until a set goal is reached. The overload principle applies to improvement of the cardiopulmonary (as well as the voluntary muscle) system. To increase efficiency of the heart and lungs, continuous rhythmic exercise (brisk walking, jogging, bicycling, swimming, or rope skipping) is ideal. Using the overload principle, increase exercise intensity gradually, until the pulse rate can be maintained at 130 for several minutes.

Programs that promise "fitness" in a minute a day are inadequate to affect circulation. So, too, are the traditionally recommended activities for the elderly, such as puttering in the garden or taking a leisurely stroll.

RATING THE FITNESS PROGRAMS

Amid all the choices for fitness programs are fads and misconceptions as well as some wise options. While some variables are dependent upon the individual, certain forms of fitness programs are of general benefit to almost everyone. Table 2–1 is a listing of how seven prominent physicians have rated the merits of 14 exercises.[7] Ratings are on a scale of 0 to 3, thus a rating of 21 indicates maximum benefit (a score of 3 by all 7 panelists). Ratings were made on the basis of regular (minimum of 4 times per week), continuous (duration of 30 minutes to one hour per session) participation in each activity.

Applying the Panel's Ratings to Older Adults

Although jogging received the highest rating by the panel, it is a taxing activity and participation must be tempered with concern for the characteristics of the older body. Generally, it is not recommended for older adults unless they have been active throughout life and jogging for several years prior to age 65. Many disorders—and mishaps—can plague the runner, including backache, kidney damage, cardiac arrest, frostbite, heat exhaustion, low blood sugar, runner's nipple, abdomen and groin muscle tears, stomach cramps, and traffic accidents. Leg and foot injuries are especially common.

Walking, which received a rating of 102, may be a reasonable alternative to jogging.

Table 2–1 Panel Rating of 14 Exercises

	Jogging	Bicycling	Swimming	Skating (ice or roller)	Handball/squash	Skiing-Nordic	Skiing-Alpine	Basketball	Tennis	Calisthenics	Walking	Golf*	Softball	Bowling
PHYSICAL FITNESS														
Cardiorespiratory endurance (Stamina)	21	19	21	18	19	19	16	19	16	10	13	8	6	5
Muscular endurance	20	18	20	17	18	19	18	17	16	13	14	8	8	5
Muscular strength	17	16	14	15	15	15	15	15	14	16	11	9	7	5
Flexibility	9	9	15	13	16	14	14	13	14	19	7	8	9	7
Balance	17	18	12	20	17	16	21	16	16	15	8	8	7	6
GENERAL WELL-BEING														
Weight control	21	20	15	17	19	17	15	19	16	12	13	6	7	5
Muscle definition	14	15	14	14	11	12	14	13	13	18	11	6	5	5
Digestion	13	12	13	11	13	12	9	10	12	11	11	7	8	7
Sleep	16	15	16	15	12	15	12	12	11	12	14	6	7	6
TOTAL	148	142	140	140	140	139	134	134	128	126	102	66*	64	51

*Ratings for golf are based on the fact that many Americans use a golf cart and/ or caddy. If one walks the links, the physical fitness value increases appreciably.

Source: Adapted from C. Carson Conrad, *How Different Sports Rate in Promoting Fitness,* U.S. Department of Health, Education, and Welfare (Washington, D.C.: U.S. Government Printing Office, 1978).

According to Consumer Guide's *Rating the Exercises:*

The best exercises for improving circulo-respiratory endurance or cardiovascular endurance are walking, jogging, swimming, dancing, bicycling and any activities that are of a continuous, dynamic nature involving large muscle groups of the body.

No one can say yet that these exercises will help you live longer, but we do know that they improve heart, health and lessen fatigue, so that you will be more productive while you are alive.[8]

Although it takes longer to achieve the same aerobic effects as jogging, walking is nearly equivalent in physiological benefit when long-term comparisons are made. (Jogging a mile in 8½ minutes burns only 26 calories more than walking a mile in 12 minutes.) Although it must be approached as a form of exercise (strolling will not do) walking is much safer and generally more enjoyable for older people. (Chapter 7 discusses the optimum walking program.)

Bicycling, like jogging, rates high in promoting fitness and well-being, although it is not recommended for busy city streets. For this reason, some have turned to the indoor stationary bicycle.

Swimming ranks third on the experts' list, with 140 points. Because swimming is a no-weight-bearing exercise, it is appropriate both for overweight individuals and those recovering from limb injuries.

According to T. Irwin, in *Family Health*, "Swimming is one of the best fitness activities around. The heart and lungs shift into heightened action, the legs and arms are used continuously and rhythmically, the back and abdominal muscles are strengthened and swimming is relaxing."[9]

As Chapter 9 explains, swimming for fitness cannot be idle splashing but should consist of a regimen of strengthening and conditioning exercises performed on a regular basis.

Ice skating is a particularly invigorating sport and it was rated highly by the panel. Skating, however, like jogging, is not recommended for adult beginners because of risk of injury. Skiing is similarly cautioned against.

Basketball may qualify as a good activity for the very fit when played at least three times a week. There are drawbacks, however: the need to find other players and, again, the risk of possible injury.

Tennis is an appropriate sport if played vigorously and frequently, yet prudently. Doubles affords appropriate cardiopulmonary stress for older individuals. Those who played in middle age will probably obtain medical approval for continuing to play as older adults.

Calisthenics, like walking, is an essential part of an older person's exercise program. Both types of exercise promote aerobic fitness, muscle tone, and a sense of well-being and are suitable to various levels of abilities (see Chapters 6 and 7 for a more complete discussion).

Golf, softball, and bowling are worth mentioning, if only to clear up the misconceptions about these sports. While they have social value and embody a "game" element that many people find stimulating, they are activities characterized more by waiting than by moving. Thus, they are not suitable as the basis for a fitness program.

Therapeutic dance, combining many elements of calisthenics and walking, is a refreshing element in a fitness program. Chapter 8 discusses in detail the merits of dance/movement therapy.

DEVICES THAT DON'T DEVELOP FITNESS

Finally, the health professional should caution patients and clients of deceptions on the market. Machines such as vibrating belts, rollers and motorized stationary bicycles do not improve muscle tone or endurance. Sauna belts, rubberized suits, and assorted garments are likewise a waste of time and money.

Saunas, whirlpools, and steambaths are pleasantly relaxing, but they are not fitness builders. Because the older person has decreased cardiovascular response to heat, they should be used only with a physician's approval.

NOTES

1. Warren R. Johnson and Charles N. Cofer, "Personality Dynamics: Psychological Implications," in *Science and Medicine of Exercise and Sport*, 2d ed., eds. Warren R. Johnson and Elsworth W. Buskirk (New York: Harper and Row, 1974), pp. 379–397.

2. Dorothy V. Harris, ed., *Women in Sports* (Washington, D.C.: American Alliance for Health, Physical Education, and Recreation, 1971), pp. 1–4.

3. Ibid.

4. H. Harrison Clarke, *Application of Measurement to Health and Physical Education* (Englewood Cliffs, N.J.: Prentice-Hall, 1974), p. 158.

5. J.M. Tanner, *Growth at Adolescence*, 2nd ed. (Springfield, Ill.: Charles C Thomas, 1962), p. 167.

6. Barbara L. Drinkwater, "Physiological Responses of Women to Exercise," in *Exercise and Sports Sciences Review*, Volume 1, ed. Jack H. Wilmore (New York: Academic Press, 1973).

7. C. Carson Conrad, *How Different Sports Rate in Promoting Fitness* (Washington, D.C.: U.S. Department of Health, Education and Welfare, U.S. Government Printing Office, 1978).

8. Charles T. Kuntzleman and the Editors of Consumer Guide, *Rating the Exercises* (New York): William Morrow and Co., 1978.

9. T. Irwin, "What Sport Is Best for You?" *Family Health,* January 1975.

Chapter 3

Psychosocial Advantages of Fitness Programs for Older People

M. Neel Buell

PERSONAL TESTIMONIES—PARTICIPATING IN FITNESS PROGRAMS

On a cold February morning, a 57-year-old woman begins a weekly ritual of sit-ups, leg lifts, and deep knee bends. After a warm-up, she and 23 other members of her exercise class proceed to such activities as floor hockey, trampoline maneuvers, and gymnastics. At 57, Mrs. G. is considered the youngster of the class, where ages more typically range from 65 to 82. This class for the elderly is sponsored by the Chicago Park District; similar programs have been started at 15 other park district gymnasiums in the city.

Meanwhile, as the Chicago program expands, other programs for the elderly are being organized around the country. Within the last three years fitness classes for older adults have been started in nearly every major American city, according to Casey Conrad, executive director of the President's Council on Physical Fitness and Sports. He regards the Chicago program as unique because of its combination of vigorous exercise and gymnastics (community-sponsored fitness programs for the elderly do not usually include gymnastics).[1]

Jane Jurew, a physical fitness instructor for the Chicago parks for 25 years, said she designed the program to be fun as well as physically therapeutic. Class members come to the gym with silver curls, paunches, and smiles and are soon engaged in animated maneuvers, racing across the floor swinging hockey sticks and shouting, "Get in there, baby!"

"The Olympics, we're not," says Ms. K., age 66. "We can't go with the Black Hawks—at least not yet," she adds with a chuckle. The women say they participate in the program to escape the loneliness of old age and for the benefits of the exercise. "Before I began exercising I had pains here," says 76-year-old Ms. Z. "Now it hurts no more."

Ms. T., who describes herself as "60 plus," could not wash her windows because of arthritis. Now she cleans them from the top step of a ladder. And Ms. R., 65, says that because of the class she can get down on her knees to clean her floors and that she can climb stairs more quickly.

One question that arose when the class began was how to balance the exercise needs of the elderly with their special problems. Ms. Jurew says she monitors the temperature of the gym floor to make sure the class members are not chilled. Her biggest concern, however, is overexertion.

"I watch for puffiness or redness in the face," she says. "I know their coloring, their ways, their breathing. If anything changes in the slightest, I know it." So far, the women have experienced no serious injuries or ill effects from the exercise program, says Ms. Jurew. In three years, the class has grown from 8 to 24 members; there is no upper age limit.

According to Dr. Robert Wiswell, isotonic exercises that tax the heart are preferable to isometric exercises (which activate muscles without movement). The best way to delay aging is to exercise vigorously. He recommends a complete physical examination to determine capacity for exercise and, if possible, to help structure the fitness program and diet.[2]

COMMON MYTHS ABOUT EXERCISING

Unfortunately, many people live more by the myths than the realities of exercise. The myths, although easier to accept, can also be damaging. Some of the more common exercise fallacies are:

- *"There's no point in exercising because it will simply increase my appetite and I'll eat back whatever I lose."* Actually, a sensible program will reduce appetite, especially if the exercise is performed just before mealtime.

- *"It takes eight hours of bike riding or jogging to lose a pound, and I simply don't have that kind of time."* Exercise is a long-range program, and it makes no sense to break it down into meaningless increments. Weight is lost over a period of time as the body is toned and strengthened both mentally and physically.

- *"I'm too old to exercise."* Prominent cardiologists and exercise physiologists urge that the benefits of exercise can be achieved at *any age* and in *no other way*. People in their 70s and 80s have literally gained a new lease on life with carefully designed exercise programs. (The same principles, incidentally, apply to youth. No one is too young to benefit from an exercise program.)

- *"I can get all the exercise I need in a few highly concentrated moments a day."* So argue the isometric advocates. Such exercises may strengthen a few limb muscles, but they do little for the most important muscle, the heart. Isometrics endangers people with high blood pressure. Static activities are not a substitute for a rational dynamic exercise program.

- *"Exercise can be done for me by machinery."* This does not work either. While certain machine exercises can strengthen injured muscles, those that claim a wide variety of conditioning benefits may force the heart rate to rise dangerously.

- *"I can lose weight in a sauna or whirlpool bath if I perspire enough, so why bother exercising?"* This is a fraud. All that is lost is water, sodium, potassium, and glucose—not one ounce of fat. Blood pressure may rise dangerously. The same objections apply to plastic sweatsuits, which foster debilitating perspiration.

The truth is, there are no shortcuts to an effective exercise program. Exercise must be performed regularly and continuously if heart function is to improve—there simply is no other way.

Regular and vigorous exercise is a stepping stone to a long, energetic life, declares Alex Comfort, author and lecturer on aging.[3] Abundant evidence supports this concept. The people of the Caucasus and Andes work hard physically throughout their long lives; it is probably one reason that many live to be over 100. (And even at 100, many are more physically fit than some urban dwellers at 20 or 30.) In the United States, farmers are among the longest living (and sedentary academicians among the shortest living) of all Americans.

PHYSIOLOGICAL BENEFITS OF EXERCISE

Why does exercise help one to live longer? In the first place, exercise helps the body resist disease-triggered aging by priming the immune system—those cells that protect against disease. Secondly, exercise improves blood circulation, keeping the body, including the brain, in tip-top condition, and helping resist primary aging.

Dr. Josef P. Hrachovec is an advocate of staying active in the later years. Regarding fitness, he says, "Exercise is the closest thing to an anti-aging pill now available. It acts like a miracle and it's free for the doing."[4]

If the human brain and body are not kept in good condition, they deteriorate rather rapidly. For instance, studies by the National Aeronautics and Space Administration show that for every three days a person is immobile, one-fifth of maximum muscle strength is lost. When 70-year-old men joined a year-long exercise program run by Dr. H.A. deVries of the University of Southern California, they developed the physical fitness attributes of healthy 40-year-olds.[5]

Historically, concern for the welfare of healthy older persons has sometimes been counterproductive. Driving them to the market when they should be walking, building shelves low when they need the opportunity for stretching, placing the TV channel selector in their laps when they should be getting out of their chairs—the list is a long one. But suffice it to say that too much is done that encourages the able-bodied oldsters to join the frail elderly prematurely.

PERSONAL TESTIMONIES—EXERCISE RESTORES THE AGING BODY

Mrs. W. is an 87-year-old woman who began a fitness program six years ago. Only five feet three inches tall and weighing 100 pounds for the past 40 years, she had developed cardiovascular disease and was treated for angina at age 67. At age 75 she was hospitalized with a severe heart attack; by age 81, she had developed an arthritic limp and had congestive heart failure, hypertension, and angina. When she began a regimen of dieting and walking at age 81, her limp limited her walking to 100 feet; the circulation in her hands was so impaired that she wore gloves in the summer to keep her hands warm.

Gradually increasing her walking, Ms. W. was able, by age 82, to be free of drugs and her previous symptoms. After four years of increased activity, she participated in the Senior Olympics in Irvine, California, where she won gold medals in the half mile and mile running events. The following year, at age 86½, she repeated the runs for another two gold medals. Each morning she runs a mile and rides her stationary bicycle 10 to 15 miles; three times weekly she works out in a gymnasium; and she follows her diet strictly. Mrs. W. is another example that age need not be a limiting factor in cardiovascular rehabilitation.

In Norwalk, California, Mr. B., a retired railroad switchman, celebrated his 90th birthday by walking 10 miles, bringing his post-retirement walking total to 135,000 miles. He is vigorous, young in spirit and heart, with a straight body and "fire in his eyes." He was not always so. He retired at 55, flabby, lame, and lethargic. His son, a physical education instructor, challenged him to "straighten out and fly right." Responding, Mr. B. began the daily regimen that now makes it possible to walk a brisk 10 miles per day.

PSYCHOSOCIAL BENEFITS OF FITNESS

Psychosocial advantages of physical fitness programs fall into three categories:

1. financial
2. social
3. emotional

Financial Aspects

Income

Money is one of the primary motivations for maintaining fitness. The older adult who is forced to retire because of declining health is faced with "diminishing dollar doldrums." For example, at an annual inflation rate of 10 percent or higher, $100 of retirement savings will be worth less than $60 within five years. On the other hand, a healthy individual of retirement age can continue working if opportunities are available or consider pursuing a new career, full or part time.

Trends indicate that mandatory retirement may soon be a thing of the past. Sixty-five was established as America's mandatory retirement age more than 50 years ago. Fifty years ago the 65-year-old person had certain general characteristics that today are more comparable to those of a man of 75 to 78, and to the woman of 80. Thus the abolition of age-fixed mandatory retirement laws is emerging as a natural consequence of increased longevity as well as the changing labor requirements.

Medical Care Expenditures

Lowering the cost of medical care is probably the greatest motivation to attain and maintain good physical fitness. High national health expenditures translate to considerable sums for older people, despite public and private health insurance plans. Casey Conrad reports that Americans spend about 10 percent of the gross national product for health care each year. Employers lose another $132 million annually to lost work days and decreased production. The fitness boom, largely a product of the past five years, is already showing results. Earlier detection of high blood pressure and improvement in diet and exercise have dropped the incidence of heart disease 15 percent. The arguments for fitness are so powerful that it is difficult to see how anyone can ignore them. Physical fitness is an idea whose time has come. The idea of survival of the fittest may be reaching a re-examination.

Dr. Madalynne Lewis, who was recently honored by Finland for her contribution to physical fitness programs, teaches fitness to older adults. Her students in Corona Del Mar, California, at the OASIS (Older Adults Social Information and Service Center) explain:

The mobility developed, the freedom from pain, the general well-being achieved by 'over sixty' citizens . . . (are) just short of a miracle.

I am 85 years old and feel that this planned exercise is helping to keep me 85 years young.

. . . the benefits to the people attending this class . . . have been considerable in lessening pain and improving the health of each of us.

I feel like a new person, all the old agility coming back.

The benefits . . . have been phenomenal. We walk straighter, at a faster pace, and move our muscles with more agility, even after only a short period.

The physical education class . . . has given us a tremendous zest for life.[6]

Ms. L. had been subject to colds all her life. At two she had whooping cough, at 13, tuberculosis, and until middle age she was afflicted by chest colds that developed into pneumonia three times. Then, at age 62, with her doctor's blessing, she started running. Now 71, she says, "After I started running I never had another cold. I've been sick once in nine years: I had a real bad flu; I had it for three hours."

Social Aspects

Social Mobility

Social mobility is the ability to seek new social experiences independently and maintaining physical fitness can help provide this independence. Perhaps the greatest benefit of maintaining physical fitness is the degree of independence it provides. The ability to plan and do things without depending on relatives, friends, or hired assistance is a significant advantage in both the financial and psychological well-being of the older person. To drive one's own car, to accomplish do-it-yourself projects, and to come and go as one pleases provide an enormous advantage.

Participation in Sporting Events

Older adults are competing in sports on a national and international level. The Senior Olympics and the U.S. Masters Track and Field Championships are outstanding examples of lifelong competition. Dr. Daniel G. Aldrich, Jr., Chancellor of the University of California at Irvine, leads a rather sedentary life much of the time, but, at age 60, he is still a fierce competitor. In the recent Pan American Masters Championships he set a new world's record for his age in the discus and threw the hammer 13 feet farther than he ever had. He says: "I enjoy participating in various sports activities and recognize good physical condition as indispensable to performing reasonably well in them."[7]

Very few adults at age 60 are concerned at how the discus is thrown, but it is important to Aldrich. And that individual satisfaction is what is important. Joan Brazil, who conducts a physical fitness program in a nursing home, said: "Physical and emotional health is important to all of us, but to the institutionalized elderly it is vital to life. Can you imagine the joy a resident feels when he can push his wheelchair for the first time with a paralyzed arm you have helped him to learn to move?"[8]

The Emeritus Institute

Less than five years ago Coastline Community College in Fountain Valley, California, established the Emeritus Institute to provide lifelong learning and self-enrichment classes for older adults. One of the first four classes offered was Adult Fitness. In the fall of 1980 the Coastline class schedule listed over 100 sections in physical education, with 48 designated for the "emeritus" or older students.[9]

Other courses at Coastline cover nutrition, dancing, and other subjects that interject fitness elements in more subtle ways. A class called Marine Intertidal Ecology is presented at the ocean in Corona Del Mar, where tidal pools contain an abundant variety of sea life. Not only do the older students develop an expertise in the identification of numerous species of marine life, they undergo a change of spirit and physical enthusiasm. Picture 20 or 30 quiet adults in their 60s, 70s, and 80s gingerly stepping off a chartered bus and heading for the beach. Watch them slowly march through ankle-deep sand and peer around or over the rocks and ledges of the tidal pool. Return with them nine weeks later to see their group having grown to more than 40 people who now shout, sing, and breathe deeply of the salty air as they literally leap through the pools. Now they scramble over and into the less accessible areas for a better look at new species. Fitness or marine biology? The students are ample evidence that the course is both.

Gladys Wolven, administrator of a convalescent center in Newport Beach, California, is very enthusiastic about the instructors at the Emeritus Institute. She observed: "The teachers who come here offer so much of themselves. I want you and them to know they are appreciated by both the residents and myself. Without them our facility wouldn't be half as pleasant and interesting as it is with our classes."[10]

Fitness Programs in Convalescent Homes

Bill Selvin was a coach and athletic director at Chapman College for several decades. Since retirement he has been "spreading the gospel" of the importance of physical fitness programs in convalescent homes. Myrna Flournoy, activity director of Beverly Manor, saw him in action. "Mr. Selvin taught 25 one-hour sessions. During this time I saw a marked and very encouraging improvement in those participating. It was easy to see they had a better self-image, and many of them remarked they were having less pain than they had prior to these classes."[11]

A testimony to the enthusiasm older people have for physical fitness programs was shown in the response to the now-famous Proposition 13 initiative in California. Loss of the state funds, which in many cases subsidized classes, reduced the summer fitness programs in California by nearly 80 percent. Concerned older people launched a letter-writing program, addressed to Senator Paul Carpenter, chairman of the State Education Committee, which led to a successful fight to reinstate classes for older adults under the banner, "Survival Skills for Seniors."[12] Nearly 7,000 students are now enrolled in the programs administered by Coastline College, with substantial numbers enrolled in other programs throughout the state and the country.

Maintaining Quality of Life

Most older people agree that longevity in itself is not the name of the game. *Quality* of life is much more important than merely delaying what is inevitable. Ten, or even just five, years of independent, healthful, vigorous living are preferable to thirty years of institutionalized vegetation.

The financial advantages of fitness maintenance are not as important in terms of saving money for medical care as are those options fitness provides for a fulfilling lifestyle. Here again the spectrum is broad— from the affluent retiree to those at the poverty-level. Nearly a million retirees in America live in adult communities such as Leisure World. Communities provide lifetime facilities for people who are able to invest $35,000 to $70,000 plus ongoing maintenance charges. Most communities have excellent fitness facilities and programs. Typically these include swimming pools, tennis courts, golf courses, and bowling greens. For those willing to use the facilities, the results can be rewarding. Fitness can become an all-consuming, positive part of the daily routine. For persons living in heterogeneous communities, the challenge to become fit is a greater one, for they must seek programs and facilities. For those who do, life has added purpose and tangible rewards.

Emotional Considerations

Several recent studies have probed the importance of fitness in the total effectiveness of the individual and in the relationship between physical fitness and psychological well-being. The research demonstrates that the individual acts and reacts as a whole, rather than as separate physical, mental, social and psychological entities. The need for exercise is clearly shown in maintaining organic soundness, in fat reduction, and in motor performance. Relationships, such as mental achievement and personal-social status, are affected by many factors, including the individual's interests, motivations, opportunities, cultural and social background as well as economic status and the influence of peers.

Consider the salient implications at least reasonably well supported by research evidence:

- A positive relationship exists between physical-motor traits and mental achievements. The general learning potential for a given level of intelligence increases in accordance with the degree of physical fitness.
- Positive relationships have been demonstrated between physical-motor traits and personal-social characteristics, as evaluated by psychological inventories, peer status indicators, teacher assessments, and self-concept evaluations.
- Participants scoring high on motor tests tend to be extroverted, dominant, sociable, dependable, tolerant, active, competitive, and popular with their peers. Those with low test scores tend to have feelings of inferiority, insecurity, and inadequacy, and have difficulties with social relationships. They are inclined to be rebellious, emotionally unstable, defensive and to have negative feelings about themselves.

Muscular tension reflects emotional states. Such states usually have been treated with drugs, which typically have some undesirable side effects. In one study, the tranquilizing effect of exercise was contrasted with the effect of 400 milligrams of meprobamate upon ten anxious men and women between 52 and 70 years of age. Muscular tension was measured by electromyography. The results showed that 15 minutes of walking at a heart rate of 100 beats per minute lowered electrical activity in the musculature by 20 percent. Neither the meprobamate nor a placebo had a significantly different effect from the exercised controls.[13] Thus, in single doses at least, exercise had significantly greater effect upon reducing tension, and without any undesirable side effects, than did the tranquilizer drug.

Studies on the psychological benefits of exercises are not new. In 1963, Cureton reviewed studies on the improvement of psychological states by means of exercise programs.[14] In one study of 500 adults a large proportion of those claiming undesirable emotional traits were relatively unfit. In another investigation personality factors correlated positively and significantly with an all-out treadmill run. Summarizing implications from his review, Cureton listed the following factors as physical correlates of personality deterioration in adults:

- accumulation of fat
- reduction in metabolic rate
- loss of muscular strength
- slowing of reaction time
- reduction in work capacity
- loss of motor fitness
- reduction in ventilation capacity
- increase in blood pressure[15]

He suggested that personality deterioration and physical deterioration paralleled each other and that improvement in physical fitness should minimize both types of deterioration.

In another study, young and old high-fit and low-fit groups of men participated in a fitness program of calisthenics, progressive running, and recreational activities for three 90-minute sessions a week over four months. Both high-fit groups were more intellectually inclined, emotionally stable, unconventional, composed, secure, easy-going, and adventurous than were the low-fit groups. The young high-fit group was more dominant and aggressive than the old high-fit group. At the end of the four-month program young and old high-fit men were more self-sufficient, and all subjects were more confident, persistent, and controlled.[16]

General Douglas MacArthur expressed some important thoughts on aging:

> Nobody grows old by merely living a number of years. People grow old only by deserting their ideals. Years may wrinkle the skin, but to give up interests wrinkles the soul. . . . Whatever your years, there is in every being's heart the love of wonder, the undaunted challenge of events, the unfailing child-like appetite for what's next, and the joy of the game of life. You are as young as your self-confidence, as old as your fear; as young as your hope, as old as your despair. In the central place of every heart there is a recording chamber; so long as it receives messages of beauty, hope, cheer and courage, you

are young. When the wires are all down and your heart is covered with the snows of pessimism and the ice of cynicism, then and only then, have you grown old.[17]

NOTES

1. President's Council on Physical Fitness and Sports, *Physical Fitness Research Digest.*

2. Robert Wiswell, personal communication.

3. Alex Comfort, personal communication.

4. Josef P. Hrachovec, *Keeping Young & Living Longer* (Los Angeles: Sherbourne Press, 1972), p. 129.

5. Herbert A. deVries, personal communication.

6. Madalynne Lewis, unpublished results from OASIS (Older Adults Social Information and Service Center), Corona Del Mar, California.

7. Daniel G. Aldrich, Jr., personal communication.

8. Joan Brazil, personal communication.

9. Emeritus Institute, Coastline Community College, Fountain Valley, California.

10. Gladys Wolven, personal communication.

11. Myrna Flournoy, personal communication.

12. Paul Carpenter, personal communication.

13. Herbert A. deVries and Gene M. Adams, "Electromyographic Comparison of Single Doses of Exercises and Meprobamate As to Effects on Muscular Relaxation." *American Journal of Physical Medicine* 51(1972): 140.

14. Thomas K. Cureton, "Improvement of Psychological States by means of Exercise Fitness Programs," *Journal of Association for Physical and Mental Rehabilitation* 7 (January-February 1963): 14–17, 25.

15. Ibid., p. 17.

16. John R. Young and A.H. Ismail, "Personality Differences of Adult Men before and after a Physical Fitness Program," October 1976.

17. Henry E. Front, "Senior Citizens, Changing the World of Leisure," *Orange Coast*, August 1979.

Rating the Programs

Thomas K. Cureton

INTRODUCTION

As fitness programs have increased in popularity in recent years, testing procedures have slowly evolved, both as teaching tools and as methods for measuring results. Chapter 4 reviews the more pertinent test results according to the type of program.

Improvements in fitness occur over time, as a "delayed reaction" to exercise. Although improvements in movement ability may be noticed quickly, fitness work also aims at more subtle physiological improvements, such as:

- improvement in basal metabolism
- circulatory and respiratory adjustments during exercise and rest
- measurable condition of the heart and arteries
- shift in blood pressure and in the blood characteristics at rest and work
- total peripheral resistance at rest and work.

Please note that the following findings are averages and intended to indicate general patterns. Individual reactions and feelings must always be used in making the final analysis for each person.

DEFINITION OF TERMS

Some factors and definitions are pertinent:

- *K-calories* refers to the number of calories used or dispensed during a given exercise.
- *Total K-calories of work* means K-calories derived from oxygen intake (liters per minute) times the length of time in minutes that the exercise lasts times 5.00.* An easy exercise would yield 50 to 100 calories per workout; moderate, 101 to 300 calories per workout; and adequate, 301 to 500 calories per workout.
- *Intensity* is the *rate* of doing the exercise (the faster the exercise, the greater the intensity). Sitting expends approximately 1 K-calorie per minute; walking, 3 to 5 K-calories per minute; jogging, 6 to 8 K-calories per minute; and very intense exercise, 10 to 15 K-calories per minute.
- *Time* is a limiting factor for people with impairments: those who are bedridden may only be able to perform 3 to 5 minutes of modified exercise; others, who are more mobile, may engage in 15 to 20 minutes of exercise. Those who have built up to a more hardy state may find they can exercise comfortably for 40 minutes.

PHYSIOLOGICAL BENEFITS OF EXERCISE

Evidence of the validity of "intervention programs" for cardiac rehabilitation is indicated by the reversals, in some instances, of deteriorative (noninfectious) disease due to therapy that includes gradual, progressive endurance exercise. Recently, very sophisticated diagnostic methods have shown improved myocardial perfusion of blood and oxygen resulting from endurance exercise.[1]

---

*This is an approximate calculation; in precise work a further, slight adjustment is made for the RQ (respiratory quotient), which is not known without actual individual measurement.

Well-designed exercise programs also combat the decline of physiological functions, which progressively degenerate with age. Past age 35, more capillaries become inactive as the maximal oxygen intake and basal metabolic rate decrease; weight and body fat progressively increase and cholesterol levels rise with weight. Various experiments have shown that exercise regimens can provide impressive improvements in motor performance functions (balance, flexibility, agility, strength, power, and endurance) and in cardiovascular and respiratory performance.

While exercise has the potential for positive change, deleterious influences on health—insufficient sleep, taking of drugs, poor nutrition, and the excessive intake of alcohol and tobacco, for example—must be minimized. The tendencies to overeat and overdrink may be lessened by good exercise programs.

RATING THE PROGRAMS

Passive Programs

Passive programs such as vibration or massage have almost no conditioning effect, many experiments show. Small, transient changes in pulse rates may result from psychological adjustments (this may be helpful to bedridden patients). The more salient findings of Kuntzleman and the editors of Consumer Guide on passive programs are:

> The sauna does not improve anyone's fitness level. It is not to be regarded as a means to achieve physical fitness. It may, however, make a contribution to relaxation and 'feeling good,' two important health objectives. . . . Elderly people and those who suffer from diabetes, heart disease, or high blood pressure should probably avoid saunas altogether.

> The sauna belt is pure hokum.

> Massage is not recommended for the development of physical fitness. Massage is effective for tension release and relief of

aching muscles, but its contribution to physical fitness is practically nil . . . Mechanical massage and vibration devices cannot reduce body weight or increase your fitness level.

Figure wrapping (generally with rubberized sweat suits) is a fraud and should be banned. It does not work and may be dangerous.[2]

Nonmotorized Stationary Bicycles

The rhythmic movement of the trunk and limbs when using a stationary bicycle has some conditioning effect. In particular, the Schwinn Ergo-Metric Exerciser (or Air-Dyne Model) is useful because it permits push-pull exercises with the arms while pedaling with the legs. Stationary cycles are particularly advantageous for people who are otherwise confined or for those who cycle regularly but cannot because of inclement weather.

Regular Calisthenics

Daily calisthenics are suitable for moderate toning and flexibility of the muscles and for moderately stimulating the heart. In the United States, the system is widely used in YMCAs, frequently followed by volleyball, swimming, or jogging. The Calisthenics for Fitness program includes running in place, jumping jacks, squat thrusts, and squat jumps. When programs are led by a competent instructor, fitness tests show some training effect based on a general regimen of 30 to 40 minutes. In one study, middle-aged men who were randomly assigned to a calisthenics group and a jogging group worked out three times a week for ten minutes over eight weeks. While physiological changes were small, the jogging group made larger improvements than the calisthenics group, especially in running endurance times and in push-ups. (A control group that did not exercise showed no change.)[3]

In general, moderate, regularly performed exercise is particularly practical and beneficial to older people for improving muscle strength and power.

Brief duration exercise programs usually have insignificant cardiovascular effects and do little to reduce serum cholesterol or fat levels. Short, intensive exercises may produce moderate reductions in pulse rates if repeated with day-to-day regularity. Such changes, however, probably result from transient tension reduction (compared with the pulse rate changes that result from longer term exercise programs, which reduce serum cholesterol, weight, and fat).

Handball

Although handball is a more vigorous form of exercise, some older people, especially those who have been playing for a long time, find it enjoyable and productive. Approximately 650 to 755 calories are expended per hour, resulting in good cardiovascular conditioning.[4]

Bowling

A person bowling continuously for an hour would expend a little less than 300 calories. As a practical matter, however, bowling is one of the most noncontinuous exercises; some estimates have calculated that an individual exercises only three minutes during an entire evening of bowling. Thus, bowling is not a productive continuous, rhythmical activity; its primary advantages are social.

Golf

Middle-aged golfers were compared with a matched group of men who engaged in the Cureton Physical Fitness Course for Adult Men. At the end of five months those who had participated in the fitness course were shown to have improved considerably more than the golfers. Consider these end-of-study test results: (1) the fitness group had a lower pulse rate (after five minutes of exercise) than the golfers (145.8/minute to 169.5/minute); (2) the fitness group outperformed the golfers in speed sit-up tests (33.82/minute to 25.60/minute); and (3) the fitness group had lower systolic blood pressure (136.6/minute to 184.6/minute). The golfers' average caloric expenditure was 196 per hour, compared to hourly expenditures for noncontinuous bowling (180), archery (168), continuous walking (334), volleyball (210), swimming (524), and jogging (679).[5]

Thus, golf, as it is now played, is not an efficient method for improving fitness. The benefits would be greater if golfers carried their own clubs and walked the course rather than rode carts.

Walking

Studies of low-intensity walking (3 to 3.5 miles an hour for one to two hours a day) indicate significant physiological changes can occur. Optimal changes result from (1) increasing distance gradually, over a period of time and (2) walking regularly, at least five days a week.

In one study, sixteen men (average age 48.9) walked three days a week for 20 weeks; a matched control group did not exercise. The walking pace of 2.5 miles per hour at the start of the experiment was gradually increased to 3.25 miles per hour. The experimental group showed these improvements: maximal respiratory volume increased from 86.9 to 102.6 liters/minute; the oxygen and pulse rate test increased from 13.8 to 17.4; resting diastolic pressure dropped nearly three millimeters; resting pulse rate, maximal exercise pulse rate, and systolic blood pressure dropped significantly; and average body weight dropped by nearly four pounds and fat levels by one percent. The control group showed no changes. Interestingly, the average walking time for the experiment subjects was only 30 minutes per day, but they learned to "put out" more energy in this time.[6]

Jogging

While jogging has become quite popular, it is not without controversy. Some view it as the ultimate conditioning method; others see no benefits and many harmful side effects. When all is said and done, jogging must be judged in individual terms, considering age, potential enjoyment, and the ability of the body to withstand the rigors of running. Too much running may lead to foot and leg disorders of a structural nature.

While most physicians discourage jogging as a new activity for the older person, it is beneficial for long-time joggers in good physical condition.

In one study, Byrd, Smith and Shackleford tested 13 men (average age 42), jogging 30 to 40 minutes a day, five days a week over 12 weeks. End-of-study testing showed that the only significant benefits were a reduction in pulse rate and an increase in maximum ventilatory rate. There were no significant reductions in fat (fat folds decreased from 18 percent to 17.2 percent; lean body mass increased 0.2 kilogram); weight (an average reduction of 1.2 pounds); or serum cholesterol levels.[7]

Another investigator tested the physiological change produced by different exercise durations. Three matched groups of men, aged 27 to 54, ran at five miles per hour, five days a week over 20 weeks. All groups performed a five-minute warm-up prior to jogging. One group jogged 15 minutes; the second, 30 minutes; and the third, 45 minutes. End-of-study testing showed that reductions in fat, total serum cholesterol, and weight were proportionate to the time spent jogging. The 15-minute group showed insignificant changes; the 30-minute group showed borderline progress; and the 45-minute group made gains that were statistically significant.[8]

Treadmill

Another study tested the efficacy of machine exercise to produce physiological change. In the study, four women used a Health Walker, a nonmotorized treadmill; a control group did not exercise. The experimental subjects exercised three times a week, in continuous, 45-minute workouts. The 45-minute period was divided into 15 minutes on the horizontal, followed by 30 minutes on a 14 percent grade. At the end of the study, the experimental group showed significant reductions in fat and significant improvements on an 18-item motor test, an agility run, and in dynamometer strength and aerobic capacity. The control group showed no change.[9]

Rowing Machine

In one study, three women exercised on a rowing machine 15 minutes a day, five days a week over eight weeks. As the weeks passed, the machine's resistance adjustments were increased, providing more strenuous upper body and leg exercise. At the same time, the rate of rowing strokes was also increased, from 20 to 28 per minute. At the end of the study, there were improvements in leg strength and in a chinning/ vertical jump and run/dipping test, as well as in tests that monitored side leg/raising and treadmill running abilities.[10]

In another study, three men (average age 60) exercised on a rowing machine 30 minutes a day, five days a week over five months. The resistance adjustment on the machine was gradually increased and the rate of strokes increased from 30 to 38 per minute. End-of-study testing showed significant fat reduction; improvements in cardiovascular, metabolic, strength, and muscular endurance tests; and systolic blood pressure reduction of 8 percent.[11]

Swimming

Swimming, considered one of the best fitness exercises, can indeed be valuable if a pool is available year-round for regular swimming.

In general, most improvements are made during the initial phase of swimming programs and reach a plateau after a year or so of participation.

Studies have found swimming to have exceptional value in developing cardiopulmonary fitness and improving total serum cholesterol and hemoglobin levels. Swimming's contribution to muscular strength is only moderate, although it develops joint flexibility and muscular endurance in the arms and shoulders.

CONCLUSIONS

Research has demonstrated that:

- Improvements in circulatory, respiratory, and metabolic (i.e., fat and weight reduction) functions are proportional to the total work done, oxygen used, and time devoted to the exercise. Programs briefer than ten minutes per day, however, generally produce insignificant changes.
- Pulse rates (while sitting, lying, standing, and exercising) generally drop as the exercise proceeds, becoming lower year after year as the exercise continues. Endurance work of one to two hours per day has a greater training effect than shorter, more intensive exercise. As the pulse rate drops, the stroke volume of the heart increases per heart beat, increasing cardiac efficiency.
- Gradual increases in quantity and/or intensity of exercise, maintained over a long period of time, yield favorable results but must be continued in order to maintain the benefits.

NOTES

1. V. Frolicher et al., "Cardiac Rehabilitation: Evidence for Improvement in Myocardial Perfusion and Function," *Archives of Physical Medicine* 61 (November 1980): 517–522.

2. Charles T. Kuntzleman and the editors of Consumer Guide, *Rating the Exercises* (New York: William Morrow and Company, 1978).

3. E. Schvartz and Tamir, "Effect of Calisthenics on Strength, Muscular Endurance and Total Body Reaction and Movement Times," *Journal of Sports Medicine and Physical Fitness* 2 (1971): 75–79.

4. F.O. Bryant, "The Effect of Handball on the Physical Fitness of Adult Men " (Master's thesis, University of Illinois, 1950).

5. Leroy H. Getchell, "An Analysis of the Effects of a Season of Golf and the Caloric Cost of Golf on Middle-Aged Men " (Ph.D. diss., University of Illinois, 1965).

6. M.L. Pollock et al., "Effect of Walking on Body Composition and Cardiovascular Function of Middle-Aged Men," *Journal of Applied Physiology* 30 (January 1971): 126–130.

7. J. Byrd, D.P. Smith and C.B. Shackleford, "Jogging in Middle-Aged Men: Effect on Cardiovascular Dynamics, *Archives of Physical Medicine and Rehabilitation* 55 (July 1974): 301–302.

8. Ali Tooshi, "Effect of Three Different Durations of Endurance Training on Serum Cholesterol, Body Composition and Other Fitness Measures" (Ph.D. diss., University of Illinois, 1970).

9. Frank J. Hayden, "The Physique and Motor Fitness Effects of Machine Exercise" (Master's thesis, University of Illinois, 1950).

10. A.E. Domke, "Conditioning Effects of Work Performed on an Exercise Machine" (Master's thesis, University of Illinois, 1955).

11. S. Molnar, "Adult Fitness Improvement and Maintenance by Progressive Rowing Machine Training " (Master's thesis, University of Illinois, 1967).

Chapter 5

Getting Started and Monitoring Progress

Leonard Biegel

Whether individual or group exercise is more desirable is open to debate. While solitude is best for one and group exercise suits another, the important element is the *doing*. Personal factors should, of course, be considered.

EXERCISING IN GROUPS

Most people, however, do derive greater advantages from exercising in groups. Consider some factors:

- *The social aspect.* Many older people are concerned with loneliness or isolation. Exercise is an excellent reason to meet others regularly.
- *The support of the group, like that found in diet and other self-improvement groups.* With the right leadership, a group can provide encouragement, increasing the advantages of the regimens. Care must be taken not to create an overtone of competition, which will either turn some people away or create undue strain. A low-key, scorekeeping method works for many, as long as individuals compete against themselves, not the group.

- *The educational aspect.* The group members (as well as the leader) are often in the best situation to provide criticism as well as praise. If it's worth doing, it's worth doing correctly.
- *Facilities.* While elaborate facilities are not required, an open, well-ventilated space is desirable, as are mats and some equipment that can be shared.
- *Group size.* Groups vary in size from 6 to 25. Larger groups should be split so that every member can participate safely.
- *Climate affects the program.* A cold climate, where there is snow and ice more than half the year, limits outdoor walking and restricts the older person's ability to travel to central points for daily fitness programs. Conversely, a predominantly hot climate may foster debilitating low energy levels, thus discouraging extended outdoor activity.

ORGANIZING THE GROUP

Group fitness programs have been organized under a number of auspices—senior centers, county or municipal recreational groups, religious center groups or clubs, and apartment building clubs, among others.

Under optimum conditions, a professional recreation specialist, physical education instructor, or physical therapist should provide overall guidance, helping to make judgments on the physical ability levels of individuals within the group. The day-to-day leader, however, can be a member of the group. In some situations, groups may find they work best by rotating leadership. This may help relieve the nervousness that some experience at the outset.

The role of the gerontologist (or other professional) is critical to the success of the program. The professional helps organize the program, defines fitness parameters, and ensures attention to individual needs (since no two people are alike nor is chronological age a clear index of a person's physical state). While generalizations regarding the physiological effects of aging are useful, individual, thorough physical examinations are basic to beginning any fitness regimen.

PRE-EXERCISE FITNESS EVALUATION

Dr. Robert E. Wear, author of Chapter 6, "Calisthenics for Active Older Individuals," offers the following "Quickie Fitness Test" for individuals who wish to form a general profile of their physical condition:

1. Do you sleep well at night or do you toss and turn and wake up snarling at the world in the morning?
2. Are you stiff and tired every morning and are your daily activities especially painful when you bend, turn, or twist?
3. Do you run out of breath climbing a flight of stairs?
4. Can you run a few yards and catch a bus without becoming exhausted?
5. Do you like looking at yourself in full-length mirrors (or do you avoid doing so)?
6. Are you proud of your appearance or have you given in to a flabby, overweight figure?
7. Does a normal day's work leave you physically exhausted? Does it take longer than it once did to recover from fatigue?
8. Do the nerves at the back of your neck go "ping" with tension before noon each day?
9. Can you walk briskly with a friend for several blocks and carry on a spirited conversation without running out of breath?
10. Do you find that you can't get to sleep at night because of tension or overtiredness and that you feel fatigued the next day?
11. Can you sit quietly and relax for a few minutes or are you constantly fidgety?
12. Has your usual mood become one of depression or pessimism, for no reason? Do you feel lonely and rejected, or are you "on top of the world" most of the time?[1]

Clearly this is not a pass-fail test, but the individual may find it enlightening.

Physicians should find the following guides (also designed by Dr. Wear) useful. The first (Exhibit 5–1) is a pre-exercise physical examina-

Exhibit 5–1 Self-Administered Pre-Exercise Questionnaire

Name ——————————————————————————————

Address ——————————————————————————————

Occupation ——————————————————————Age ————

Telephone ——————————————————————Date ————

To Be Answered by Participant	Yes	No
1. Have you ever had a heart attack (coronary thrombosis or myocardial infarction)?	——	——
2. Have you ever been told by a doctor that you have high blood pressure, a heart murmur, or heart disease?	——	——
3. Is your heart beat ever irregular, or are there spells when it suddenly quickens?	——	——
4. Are you taking digitalis, quinidine, nitroglycerine or any other medication?	——	——
5. Are you taking any other medication prescribed by a physician at the present time?	——	——
6. Do you ever have chest pains on vigorous exertion?	——	——
7. If you walked on level ground for a mile at an average pace, would you become out of breath, have pains in your chest or legs, or develop marked fatigue?	——	——
8. Have you ever had lung disease?	——	——
9. Do you have diabetes?	——	——
10. Do you have gout, arthritis, or rheumatism?	——	——
11. Do you have any disabilities of the feet, ankles, knees, hips, or back?	——	——
12. Do you have a rupture or hernia?	——	——
13. If you are under the care of a physician, does your physician approve of your entering a physical fitness program?	——	——
14. Do you have any illness at the present time? If "yes," describe: ———————————	——	——

—————————————————————————————

—————————————————————————————

15. Please list any operations or serious illnesses that you have had in the last five years: ———————————

—————————————————————————————

—————————————————————————————

—————————————————————————————

—————————————————————————————

Source: Adapted from Robert E. Wear, *Fitness, Vitality, and You* (Durham: New Hampshire Council on the Aging/New England Gerontology Center).

tion guide; the second (Exhibit 5–2), a basic form for a consent letter. It is, of course, incumbent upon the physician, in filling out the consent letter, to be thoroughly familiar with the program being approved.

The program organizer will generally find that the group falls into several categories:

- those in generally good health, who have exercised for many years and continue to do so;
- those in generally good health but who lead sedentary lives, with no regular fitness regimen; and
- those who, for one reason or another, must restrict the strenuousness of their fitness program.

With proper leadership, individuals on all three levels can work together in a fitness program.

Exhibit 5–2 Basic Form of Consent Letter

                                          _____

                                             Date

Dear _____:

My patient, _____, may participate in the specially designed low-level program for older adults at the _____.

Patient's Age _____ Weight _____ Height _____

Smoking Habits _____

Physician—Please note any contraindications or special instructions. Also indicate what, if any, medication the patient is now taking: _____

_____

_____

_____

_____

Source: Adapted from Robert E. Wear, *Fitness, Vitality, and You* (Durham: New Hampshire Council on the Aging/New England Gerontology Center).

THE FIRST MEETING

An effective way to begin a program is with an organizing meeting to which a broad invitation has been extended. It is important, at such a meeting, to listen to everyone's views about themselves, and to make attendees comfortable. It is particularly useful, at this stage, to dispel myths and misconceptions. To this end, the leader should summarize basic information on the aging process and how it is affected by exercising.

LIFESTYLE INVENTORY

Seemingly unrelated information can be brought into focus at the meeting, leading to a discussion of lifestyle habits. This is a good way to alert individuals to weaknesses and strengths in their own daily routines. The Public Health Service's Office of Disease Prevention and Health Promotion offers an interesting and useful lifestyle inventory (see Exhibits 5–3 and 5–4).

Exhibit 5–3 Lifestyle Inventory—Smoking Habits

	Almost Always	Sometimes	Almost Never
1. If the individual never smokes, enter a score of 10 for this section and go to the section on alcohol and drug intake.			
2. Avoids smoking cigarettes.	2	1	0
3. Smokes only low tar-and-nicotine cigarettes, a pipe, or cigars.	2	1	0
Total			

Exhibit 5–4 Lifestyle Inventory—Alcohol and Drug Intake

	Almost Always	Sometimes	Almost Never
1. If the individual avoids drinking alcoholic beverages or has no more than one or two drinks a day.	4	1	0
2. Avoids using alcohol or other drugs as a way of handling stressful situations.	2	1	0
3. Is careful not to drink alcohol when taking certain medicines (for example, medicine for sleeping, pain, colds, and allergies).	2	1	0
4. Reads and follows the label directions when using prescribed and over-the-counter drugs.	2	1	0
Total			

A general interpretation of the responses:

- *Scores of 9 and 10.* This individual understands the importance of this area to good health. As long as current practices continue, this area should not pose a health risk.
- *Scores of 6 to 8.* Health practices in this area are good, but there is room for improvement. The individual should look at the items answered "sometimes" or "almost never." What changes can be made to improve the score?
- *Scores of 3 to 5.* Health risks are showing! Perhaps the individual needs help making choices.
- *Scores of 0 to 2.* This individual is taking serious and unnecessary health risks. Perhaps he or she is not aware of the risks and/ or what to do about them.

DESIGNING THE EXERCISE PROGRAM

The next step comes in analyzing the health and lifestyle of each group member, along with physical or logistical limitations. It is important to start slowly with a regular program, exercising half an hour a day, seven days a week. For most people, meeting under the auspices of a senior center program, a 5-day program can generally be the norm, supplemented informally by individual or informal group work on the weekends. It is important to remember that individual variations will be present in almost every group. These variations will require the group to be informally divided into capability groupings. In such cases, the less advanced will stop their activities sooner than the more advanced. The astute group leader should use these differences as an inspiration for the less advanced and should remember to praise each individual's progress. The following is an example of a workable program:

Monday	Calisthenics
Tuesday	Walking
Wednesday	Calisthenics
Thursday	Swimming
Friday	Dancing
Saturday	Calisthenics
Sunday	Walking

A different mix of activities can work just as well; the important factor is to maintain variety.

What time of day to exercise is a further consideration. The resounding recommendation of most experts is that the morning (at least one and one-half hours after breakfast and before lunch) is best. While this may vary to meet special circumstances, no one should ever exercise immediately after eating.

ANALYZING RESULTS

Five or six weeks after the start of an exercise program, it is appropriate to begin a regular, periodic review of the results. By this time, those who required gradual conditioning as well as those who needed to learn exercise patterns should be noticing the first results. Once a review process is started, it should be conducted at weekly intervals. Individuals should find that this measurement is important to their physical well-being as well as to morale.

A simple preprogram test, such as the "Quickie Fitness Test," detailed earlier in this chapter, can be administered again at the outset of the review process. Test results can be logged thereafter, correlating the results with quantity and duration of exercise performed.

Interpreting results should not be limited, however, to filling out charts and forms and questionnaires. Discussion is also valuable, both to do away with lingering anxieties about exercise and to learn what others are doing. Informal discussions will likely occur between the more congenial members of the group; more formal discussions should be scheduled weekly and should last approximately one-half hour.

NOTE

1. Robert E. Wear, personal communication.

Chapter 6

Calisthenics for Active Older Individuals

Robert E. Wear

INTRODUCTION

The exercises given in this chapter were designed for a variety of physical positions, from sitting to lying to standing.

Each exercise is suitable for individual conditioning or group participation and is categorized by function (i.e., area of the body to be exercised). The participant should, in each case, begin slowly, with two or three repetitions at first, and build to a specified number over several weeks.

Older adults should start by doing a few minutes of simple exercises at least four or five times a week. The exercise program should be a regular part of one's daily routine and should be scheduled for the same time each day. Needless to say, exercise should not be done immediately after eating. Mid to late morning is an ideal time.

GOALS

The exercises recommended here are intended to:

- increase range of motion (not produce muscle soreness)
- improve peripheral circulation (the movement of blood in the arms, legs, hands, and feet), not overtax the heart

61

- improve the body's ability to withstand stress (not cause prolonged fatigue).

While calisthenics are not a complete fitness program for many people, they are an important warm-up activity for more intense cardiopulmonary activities such as swimming, walking, and bicycling.

Within each category, there is no special order to follow. However, the vigorous standing activities should be preceded by easy walking, chair, or floor activities for five to ten minutes to ease the body into the greater exertion.

GENERAL GUIDELINES

The following are some ground rules for the exercise leader (they are also valid for the individual exercising alone):

- While there is no special order, individuals should follow a routine that is enjoyable and easy to remember, while at the same time exercising as many muscles and joints as possible. One should concentrate mostly on the muscles that hold the body upright. The ankle, knee, back, and abdominal muscles should be exercised because they undergo the most gravitational stress. For many it works well to start with the leg exercises first, because the legs are generally stronger than other parts of the body. Gradually, exercises involving the arms and shoulders can be integrated into the program.
- Exercise routines should start with some of the easy warm-ups detailed in this chapter.
- Individuals should start each activity at their own pace, with only a few repetitions, especially during the initial days of conditioning. As strength, endurance, and flexibility increase, they will be able to exercise for longer periods with greater ease. A maximum of ten repetitions is generally the rule before proceeding to a new activity.

- Exercise as little as ten or fifteen minutes during the first few sessions. Individuals have had a lifetime to acquire their present shape and condition; it takes time to make positive changes. Body movements should be fun, not grueling. One should quit when pleasantly tired and try a little more next time.

- Move easily from one activity to another without interruption or loss of time.

- Avoid muscle fatigue and soreness by not performing exercises more than twice in succession that would stress the muscles of one joint. Use other areas of the body and return to that joint later.

- Body positions should be changed at regular intervals—from front to side to back and on all fours, to standing and kneeling. Variation is the spice of exercise.

- It is perfectly normal to experience heart pounding and heavy breathing after exercising; however, these symptoms should not continue for more than a few minutes once the exercise has ended.

- Breathe naturally through the mouth and nose to get the oxygen needed; never hold the breath. If one is exercising hard, one should breathe in hard and exhale forcefully.

- Try to swing free! Individuals who jerk and bob to touch their toes with locked knees may be unable to straighten up without intense back pain. Bouncing and jerking merely increase stiffness and soreness; therefore, movements should be kept smooth and simple. Knees should be bent, hips flexed, the trunk rotated, and arms swung in a natural, comfortable manner. Each person should follow a personal tempo, moving with relaxed body rhythm, and staying within individual limitations. Do not try to keep up with other members of the group if the activity is too difficult or the pace too fast.

- Individuals should be sure to get enough sleep and rest between exercise periods; the body needs time to recover from muscle fatigue, to remove waste products, and to rebuild muscle tissue. Naturally, the muscles being exercised will ache a bit but if the pain persists, exercise less strenuously, until each movement can be handled with ease.

INCORPORATING EXERCISE INTO EVERYDAY ACTIVITY

Dr. Arthur Steinhaus, former dean of George William College, gives these general tips for incorporating exercise into everyday activities:

- Always stand when dressing or undressing.
- Park the car or get off the bus or train a few blocks from your destination and briskly walk the rest of the way.
- Avoid using the elevator or escalator to go up or down two or three floors. If you must take the elevator, get off on the wrong floor and walk two or three flights.
- Take a brisk walk around the block in the morning and evening.
- Look for opportunities to bend and stretch while gardening.
- Sweep with brisk, vigorous motions.[1]

Added to Dr. Steinhaus' hints are:

- Remember good posture at all times: stand, walk, and sit tall!
- Don't be afraid to use some kind of support when beginning an exercise program. At first, standing unsteadily out on the floor can be an unsettling experience. Exercise in a sitting position or hold on to chairs, railings, or sturdy furniture for support.

ADDITIONAL NOTES OF CAUTION AND PRECAUTION

- A week's worth of exercise should not be squeezed into a day. Spread the exercise sessions regularly throughout the week and enjoy each day's exercise at a time.
- Avoid closing the eyes during exercise. A loss of balance and a possible fall may be the result.

- Under no circumstances go directly into a sauna or steam bath after exercising. During intense activity, the heart works hard to supply the body with blood for oxygen delivery, supplying blood sugars and fats, removal of waste products, and cooling of an overheated system. The extra burden of cooling an already hot body in an extreme heat situation may impose an undue burden on the cardiovascular system, with possibly serious complications.
- Don't underestimate the capacity to exercise. The body is capable of definite individualized fitness improvement if intensity and duration of exercise are not increased too rapidly. The body improves (and declines) at its own rate.
- The rate of perspiration is no indication of the training value of the exercise program. (People perspire at different rates and in different amounts.) Therefore, proceed in exercise routines at a sensible and graduated intensity, duration, and frequency.
- Avoid performing an exercise until it is certain that the exercise is beneficial. If there is pain or discomfort, consult a physician.
- Don't begin a vigorous exercise program until completing a thorough physical examination and discussing the activity plan with a knowledgeable doctor.
- Avoid rubberized, plastic, or too-tight clothing. Restraining garments restrict ventilation, elevate body temperature, cause profuse sweating, and do not significantly change body weight loss.

SPECIFIC PROGRAMS

The remainder of the chapter is concerned with four exercise programs for individuals at various levels of conditioning—from the unconditioned sedentary to the fit marathoner. These programs are:

1. Rhythmic Movements in a Sitting Position
2. Vigorous Chair-Supported Activities
3. Vigorous Floor Activities
4. Vigorous Standing Activities.

Rhythmic Movements in a Sitting Position

General Information

These exercises are designed to tone up unused muscles and tendons and to increase strength and range of motion. As the individual progressively completes the different routines, balance, coordination, and circulation in the hands and feet should improve.

The sitting exercises are, in most cases, well suited to people confined to sitting positions. Fully mobile people may wish to use the sitting exercises to begin a daily routine, as a prelude to more intensive exercises. These exercises may also be beneficial for stretching and relief of tension, regardless of a person's level of mobility. They should be performed using a well-balanced chair with arms and with rubber tips on the legs to prevent sliding.

Each exercise should be started with a few repetitions—only two, three, or four at first—and increased during a period of several weeks to not more than ten repetitions of each movement during an exercise period. (See Exhibit 6–1 for a summary listing of rhythmic movements in a sitting position.)

Part I: Easy Warm-ups

1. Hands up
   Objective: To strengthen and loosen arms, shoulders, and upper torso in preparation for further movement.
   Exercise Progression:
   a. Sit in an upright position.
   b. Raise both arms overhead toward the ceiling. Reach as high as possible and hold for three seconds.
   c. Lower arms and let them hang at sides. Repeat the entire movement three times.
2. High Stepping
   Objective: To rhythmically lift the legs and feet in big muscle movement to warm up and loosen lower extremities.
   Exercise Progression:
   a. Sit upright with hands resting on thighs.

Exhibit 6–1 Rhythmic Movements in a Sitting Position

Exercise Number	Title	Brief Description	Beginning Number of Repetitions
1.	Hands up	Both hands reach high overhead	3
2.	High Stepping	March in place, lifting knees	10–15 seconds
3.	Yes	Move head up and down slowly	4
4.	No	Move head from side to side slowly	4
5.	Maybe	Slowly bend head alternately to each shoulder	4
6.	I Don't Know	Slow lifting and lowering shoulder shrugs	4
7.	Side Rock	Bend to opposite sides of body with both hands	4
8.	Knee Grabber	Lift knees alternately to chest	4
9.	Shoulder Rotations	Shoulder shrugging action, forward and backward	6, each way
10.	Row Your Boat	Bend, reach forward, and pull arms back	6
11.	Tail Lift	Hold seat of chair and lift hips upward	4
12.	Ankle Circles	Cross legs and rotate feet at ankles	10, each way
13.	Crawl Stroke	Alternate arm pull as in crawl swimming	5
14.	Wrist Circles	Grasp wrist and circle extended hand clockwise and counterclockwise	6
15.	Hocus-Pokus	Forceful thrust of arms with finger spread	6
16.	Knee Squeezers	Alternate push and press action of knees against hand resistance	4
17.	Slump ups	Alternately slump into chair and then sit up	4
18.	Toe Touches	Sit and reach for right toe, between legs, and then left toe	3–5

Exhibit 6–1 continued

19.	Oriental Bows	Bend forward at waist, arms swing back and up	2
20.	Reach out	Stretch arms out to the side, hold, and drop	2
21.	Shake It Loose	Alternately lift each leg, bend knee, and shake legs gently	2, each leg

    b. Lift right thigh as high as possible while pointing toes toward the floor. Return foot to the floor.

    c. Now lift the left thigh high and return it to the floor. Repeat entire movement ten times, maintaining a rhythm as if marching. Bouncy marching music will aid in the rhythm of this exercise.

  3. Yes

Objective: To stretch and tone the muscles of the front and back of the neck in a slow forward and backward movement.

Exercise Progression:

    a. Sit in an erect position with head held high.

    b. Slowly drop head forward, placing chin on chest.

    c. Slowly draw head back as far as possible. This movement is just like its name. One is moving the head as if nodding "Yes." Repeat movement four times in each direction and progress to ten repetitions.

  4. No

Objective: To stretch and tone the muscles at the side of the neck and upper back.

Exercise Progression:

    a. Sit in an erect position with head held high.

    b. Slowly turn head to look over the right shoulder.

    c. Slowly turn head to look over the left shoulder. In this exercise one should move the head as if slowly shaking the head to say "No." Repeat movement four times in each direction and progress to ten repetitions.

5. Maybe
   Objective: To stretch and tone the muscles at the side of the neck.
   Exercise Progression:
   a. Sit in an erect position with head held high. Cross arms across chest with hands on shoulders.
   b. Slowly bend the head to the left side, reaching toward the left shoulder with the left ear. Touch the left ear to the right hand. Do not lift the shoulder to the ear—stretch the neck and make it do the work. Repeat the movement four times in each direction and progress to ten repetitions.
6. I Don't Know
   Objective: To strengthen and help reduce tension in the upper shoulder and lower neck region.
   Exercise Progression:
   a. Sit in an erect position with the head held high and arms hanging at the sides.
   b. Shrug or lift both shoulders up toward the ears. Now drop them to a relaxed position. Repeat this movement five times, eventually progressing to ten repetitions.
7. Side Rock
   Objective: To twist, stretch, and loosen the side, trunk and abdominal muscles.
   Exercise Progression:
   a. Sit in an erect position with head held high.
   b. Slowly bend the body to the right, reaching toward the floor with both hands. Hold this position for three seconds. Now return to the upright position.
   c. Repeat the movement on both sides until it has been done four times.

Part II: More Vigorous Activities

8. Knee Grabber
   Objective: To strengthen the thigh muscles and hip flexors and to stretch the muscles of the lower back, buttocks, and back of the legs.
   Exercise Progression:
   a. Sit straight with both hands holding the right knee.

b. Raise the right knee toward the chest. Press the knee toward the head with hands while forcefully exhaling. Slowly lower the right leg while inhaling.

c. Repeat the same movement with the left leg, being sure to exhale on pressure of the knee to the head. Repeat four times and progress to eight repetitions with each leg.

9. Shoulder Rotations

Objective: To strengthen and loosen the muscles of the shoulder girdle.

Exercise Progression:

a. Sit in an erect position with arms hanging by the sides and the head held high.

b. Lift the shoulders in a shrugging action. Rotate the shoulders backward, making a large circle.

c. Now reverse the direction, rotating the shoulders forward. Repeat six times and progress to ten repetitions in each direction.

10. Row, Row, Row Your Boat

Objective: To stretch and loosen the muscles of the back, arms, and shoulders.

Exercise Progression:

a. Sit in an erect position with arms extended at shoulder height in front of the body.

b. Bend forward, while stretching the arms and shoulders.

c. Slowly pull the arms back toward the body while returning to an upright position. This action is similar to rowing a boat. Repeat the movement five or six times and progress to ten repetitions.

11. Tail Lift

Objective: To strengthen the arms, shoulders, and back and to stretch the trunk and hips.

Exercise Progression:

a. Sit in an erect position on the front edge of a sturdy chair, with the hands holding the sides of the seat slightly behind the buttocks. The knees should be flexed 90 degrees with the feet flat on the floor.

b. Raise the hips off the chair while pushing the head back and looking at the ceiling. Straighten the body at the hips and hold this position for three or four seconds. Return to the starting position. This is a vigorous movement; therefore, repeat it only three more times at first, gradually building up to five or six repetitions.

12. Ankle Circles
    Objective: To increase the flexibility of the ankles and to stretch the muscles of the lower legs.
    Exercise Progression:
    a. Sit in an erect position and cross the right leg over the left leg with the right foot hanging in a relaxed position.
    b. Rotate the right foot, making the largest circle possible with the toes in a clockwise direction. Forcefully turn the foot inward.
    c. Next, lift the right toes as high as possible toward the ankle.
    d. Now rotate the right toe and foot outward before completing the circle and returning to the starting position. Repeat in a counterclockwise manner. Repeat five circles with the right foot. Change leg positions, left over right, and repeat the circle five times with the left foot in clockwise and counterclockwise directions. Progress to ten circles with each foot and ankle in each direction.

13. The Crawl Stroke
    Objective: To strengthen and increase the stamina and flexibility of elbow and shoulder joints.
    Exercise Progression:
    a. Sit in an erect position with both arms extended at shoulder height in front of the body.
    b. Pull the right hand downward toward hip while bending the elbow upward and away from the body.
    c. Repeat the same movement with the left hand and elbow. This movement is similar to an overhead crawl stroke. Repeat five complete strokes and progress to no more than 25 repetitions at any one time.

14. Wrist Circles
    Objective: To strengthen and limber the wrists.
    Exercise Progression:
    a. Grasp the right wrist with the left hand. The palm of the right hand should face downward.

b. Slowly rotate the right hand upward and outward in a clockwise circle movement.

c. Continue making the largest circle possible, moving the hand into a downward position.

d. Return the hand to the starting position. After several repetitions, reverse to a counterclockwise direction. Now grasp the left wrist with the right hand and repeat the circling movements with the left hand. Repeat five times in each direction (with both hands) and progress to ten repetitions in each direction with both hands.

15. Hocus-Pokus (Open and Closed Fist Movements)

Objective: To strengthen the muscles of the forearms and increase the flexibility of the fingers.

Exercise Progression:

a. Sit with hands closed in a fist, close to the chest.

b. While extending the arms forward, open and close the fingers.

c. Repeat this movement five times and progress to ten repetitions.

16. Knee Squeezers

Objective: To strengthen the muscles on the inside and outside of the thighs and increase the endurance of the arms and shoulders.

Exercise Progression:

a. Sit in an erect position with the knees close together and feet flat on the floor. Place the hands on the outside of the knees.

b. Forcefully separate the knees against the resistance of the hands to a slow count of five.

c. With knees in the separated position, place hands on the inside of the knees. Push the knees together against the resistance of the hands to a slow count of five. Repeat three times and progress to eight repetitions in each direction.

17. Slump ups

Objective: To tone the abdominal muscles and strengthen the muscles of the lower back.

Exercise Progression:
a. Sit in an erect position at the front edge of a sturdy chair, with hands on thighs. The knees should be flexed 90 degrees with the feet flat on the floor.
b. Relax the back muscles and slump into the chair by curving the back and resting the chin on the chest.
c. Tighten the back muscles to return to a straight position. Repeat three more times and progress to ten repetitions.

18. Toe Touches
    Objective: To stretch and limber the muscles of the back.
    Exercise Progression:
    a. Sit in an erect position with the feet flat on the floor, legs spread and hands on knees.
    b. Bend forward at the waist and extend fingers beyond right toes.
    c. Return to the starting position.
    d. Extend fingers between the legs.
    e. Return to the starting position.
    f. Extend fingers beyond left toes.
    g. Return to the starting position. Repeat the three stretching actions five times. Progress to ten repetitions.

Part III: Cool-down Movements

19. Oriental Bows
    Objective: To stretch and loosen the muscles of the back and shoulders.
    Exercise Progression:
    a. Sit in a comfortable upright position.
    b. Relax the back by bending forward at the waist. Reach toward the floor with both hands and lower the chin toward the knees. Hold this position for three to four seconds, then return to the upright position. Repeat the entire movement one more time.

20. Reach out
    Objective: To lift, stretch, and then relax the upper arm and shoulder muscles at the shoulder joint.

Exercise Progression:
a. Sit in a comfortable upright position.
b. Extend the arms to the sides at shoulder height. Stretch the arms away from the body as far as possible. Hold this position for three seconds.
c. Now relax the arms and let them hang loosely at the sides. Repeat the entire movement one more time.
21. Shake It Loose
Objective: To stretch and loosen the muscles of the upper and lower leg.
Exercise Progression:
a. Sit in a comfortable upright position with hands on the thighs.
b. Take five deep breaths, exhaling slowly each time.
c. Lift and slightly extend the right leg, with the toes several inches off the floor. Relax the leg and shake it gently for three or four seconds.
d. Now let both arms hang loosely at the sides and shake gently for three or four seconds. Repeat the same movements with the left leg and repeat exercise once more.

Progression to Greater Mobility and Endurance

Those who can progress to more vigorous exercises have now stretched and loosened up and are ready to proceed. The following chair-supported and floor exercises are easy and enjoyable and should be done without straining. Participants should learn to relax between movements and to benefit the entire body by trying each exercise.

Vigorous Chair-Supported Activities

These exercises are intended to:

• strengthen and stretch abdominal, chest, and back muscles
• stretch the ankles and legs and strengthen the calves and thighs
• loosen the hamstring muscles in back of the thighs and tighten the buttocks

- release tension in the arms, shoulders, and back
- stretch and strengthen the arms and shoulders.

Chairs are excellent props or stable supports for a wide variety of movements. At first try these movements to music, with a slow, easy rhythm. Later, increase the tempo as proficiency increases. Keep the number of repetitions low in the beginning and progress to a maximum of ten. Exhibit 6–2 is a summary listing of the vigorous chair-supported activities.

1. One-Arm Overhead Stretcher
   Objective: To stretch the muscles of the lower back, chest and shoulders.
   Exercise Progression:
   a. Stand erect behind a chair, with the left hand resting on the chair back and the right arm straight overhead.

Exhibit 6–2 Vigorous Chair-Supported Activities

Exercise Number	Title	Brief Description	Beginning Number of Repetitions
1.	One-Arm Overhead Stretcher	Hold chair back, lift each arm, and stretch.	4, each arm
2.	Inside Leg Swing	With chair support, swing inside leg forward and backward. Reverse body and leg positions.	6, each leg
3.	Heel Raise to Drop Seat	Lift heels and move to a half knee bend drop seat position.	4
4.	Limber up	Grasp chair arms. Move from a front leaning rest to an extended body stretch.	2
5.	Arm Chair Push-ups	With arms extended, grasp chair arms. Bend forward and push back.	2

b. Reach overhead with the right hand, keeping the arm straight and the eyes looking forward. Return to the starting position. Repeat three times with each arm.

2. Inside Leg Swing
Objective: To limber the upper thigh, lower back, and hip muscles.
Exercise Progression:
a. Stand to the left of a chair, with the right hand resting on the left side of the chair back. Keep the feet together.
b. Swing the right leg forward as far as comfortable, balancing on the left leg and the right hand.
c. Swing the right leg backward comfortably, then swing it forward. Repeat the swinging movement four or five times.
d. Step to the right, hold the chair with the left hand, and swing the left leg forward and back in the same manner.

3. Heel Raise to Drop Seat
Objective: To strengthen the muscles of the feet, legs, thighs, and lower back.
Exercise Progression:
a. Stand two feet in front of a chair. Grasp the arms of the chair while leaning forward.
b. Lift heels up and drop head.
c. Keeping the head lowered, bend knees and do a half knee bend to a drop seat position. Return to the starting stance. Repeat only three or four times at first before progressing to a maximum of ten repetitions.

4. Limber up
Objective: To limber the back and stretch the shoulder and leg muscles.
Exercise Progression:
a. Stand two feet in front of a chair. Grasp the arms of the chair.
b. Drop the head and chest into a deep forward bending position.
c. Swing upward, raising the head and arching the body in a front leaning position. Return to the starting position. Repeat the sequence two or three times and progress to five or six repetitions.

5. Arm Chair Push-ups
   Objective: To improve strength and endurance of the arm, shoulder, and chest muscles.
   Exercise Progression:
   a. Stand approximately three feet in front of a sturdy chair, legs together. Keeping the head erect, grasp the arms of the chair, making sure that chair and feet are firmly anchored so they will not slip.
   b. Slowly lower the chest toward the chair, keeping the back straight. Straighten the arms and push body back to the starting position. This is a vigorous exercise and only one or two repetitions should be attempted at first. As strength and endurance increase, gradually work toward continuous sequences.

Vigorous Floor Activities

These exercises are intended to:

- strengthen and stretch the muscles of the abdomen, trunk, and lower back
- tighten and strengthen the muscles of the lower leg and anterior and posterior thigh
- loosen the hamstring muscles in the back of the thigh and tighten the buttocks
- strengthen and stretch the muscles of the arms and shoulders
- release tension in the muscles of the back, shoulders, and arms.

Exhibit 6–3 is a summary listing of the vigorous floor activities.

1. Knee to Chin
   Objective: To stretch the muscles of the lower back, calves, and buttocks and strengthen the muscles of the neck, shoulders, and arms.
   Exercise Progression:
   a. Lie on the back with legs together and arms at the sides.

Exhibit 6–3 Vigorous Floor Activities

Exercise Number	Title	Brief Description	Beginning Number of Repetitions
1.	Knee to Chin	Back lying position. Pull right knee to head. Repeat with left knee.	4
2.	Bicycling in the Air	Back lying position. Lift legs and do bicycling motion slowly.	10 cycles
3.	Backward Body Bridge	Sitting to back extended position. Hold and return.	3
4.	Side Leg Lifts	Side lying position. Alternately raise and lower top leg. Reverse body position and repeat.	3, each side
5.	Head and Shoulder Curl	Back lying position to front abdominal curl-up and return.	3
6.	Alternate Arm Lifts	Prone position. Alternately lift straight arms off the floor.	3
7.	Hip Twister	Back lying, arms outstretched position. Alternately roll hips to right and left.	5, each side
8.	Angry Cat— Swayback Horse	All fours kneeling position. Arch back, then move to a swayback position.	3
9.	Log Roller	Fully extended, back lying position. Roll body from front to side to back to front.	5
10.	Mule Kicking	Hands and knees position. Swing left knee to chest, then kick back. Alternate with right leg.	3, each leg
11.	Rocking Chair	Sitting position. Rock backward to upper shoulder position and return.	5
12.	Tail Wag	Hands and knees position. Swing hips and head alternately to right and left.	8
13.	Swing Back Stretcher	Hands and knees position. Forward lean to backward extension position.	3

   b. Grasp the right knee with both hands and pull knee toward chin. Raise the head and shoulders off the floor. Return to the starting position.

   c. Repeat with the left knee and then repeat three more times with each knee. Progress to eight to ten repetitions.

2. Bicycling in the Air
   Objective: To limber the upper leg and hip muscles and improve endurance of the front hip and abdominal muscles.
   Exercise Progression:
   a. Lie on the back, with knees bent and feet flat on the floor. The arms should be at the sides, palms down.
   b. Raise the feet off the floor.
   c. Begin a slow bicycling motion with both legs. Point the toes. Make ten cycling motions and return to the starting position.

3. Backward Body Bridge
   Objective: To stretch the upper shoulders and to strengthen the muscles of the back, buttocks, thighs, and legs.
   Exercise Progression:
   a. Sit with the hands behind and slightly to the side of trunk. Keep the legs straight and fully extended.
   b. Raise the buttocks off the floor until the hips are as straight as possible. Move the head back to look toward the ceiling. Hold this position for three seconds. Return to the starting position. Repeat two more times; eventually progress to five or six repetitions.

4. Side Leg Lifts
   Objective: To strengthen and stretch the muscles of the trunk and on the outside and inside of the thighs.
   Exercise Progression:
   a. Lie on the left side with the head resting on the left. Keep the back straight. The right hand rests on the floor in front of the waist for balance.
   b. Raise the right leg as far as possible without straining. Point the toes and keep the knees straight. Lower the leg to the starting position. Repeat this movement three times on the left side and three times on the right side. Gradually increase repetitions to ten on each side.

5. Head and Shoulder Curl

    Objective: To strengthen the abdominal muscles.

    Exercise Progression:

    a. Lie on the back with legs together and hands resting on top of the thighs.
    b. Moving slowly, raise the chin toward the chest while reaching toward the knees with the fingers. (Don't strain to touch fingers to knees; this will become easier with time.) Exhale and tense the abdominal muscles while curling.
    c. Slowly return to the back lying position. Repeat three times at first, gradually building to ten repetitions.

6. Alternate Arm Lifts

    Objective: To strengthen the back and shoulder muscles and stretch the chest muscles.

    Exercise Progression:

    a. Lie on the abdomen with arms and legs fully extended.
    b. Keeping the elbows straight, lift the left arm off the floor. Lift the head, looking up as high as possible without straining. Return the arm to the floor.
    c. Stretch the right arm up and return to original position. Repeat three times, alternating arms, and progress to ten repetitions with each arm.

7. Hip Twister

    Objective: To stretch and limber the muscles of the lower trunk.

    Exercise Progression:

    a. Lie on the back with arms outstretched to each side at shoulder level, palms down. Keep knees bent and feet flat on the floor.
    b. Roll hips to the left and return to the starting position.
    c. Now roll the hips to the right. Try to keep the fingers touching the mat while rotating the hips. Start with five rotations to the right and five to the left, gradually progressing to ten on each side.

8. Angry Cat—Swayback Horse

    Objective: To strengthen the abdominal and back muscles and to reduce tension in the lower back.

Exercise Progression:

a. Start in the "all fours" kneeling position with elbows straight, head up, and the back flat.

b. Arch the back upward by tensing the abdominal muscles. Lower the head between arms and exhale forcefully. Hold this position for three seconds.

c. Now relax into a swayback position and lift the head. Inhale. Return to the starting position. Repeat three times and progress to ten repetitions.

9. Log Roller

Objective: To stretch the muscles of the trunk, arms, and legs.

Exercise Progression:

a. Lie on the back with arms outstretched overhead and legs fully extended.

b. Slowly roll to the right side, keeping the body fully stretched.

c. Continue rolling, onto the chest. Keep arms and legs as straight as possible. Reverse, rolling to the left onto the chest. Repeat the movement four or five times from front to back and reverse.

10. Mule Kicking

Objective: To strengthen and stretch the muscles of the lower back, buttocks, and posterior thighs.

Exercise Progression:

a. Start in the "all fours" kneeling position, with elbows straight and head up.

b. Forcefully swing the left knee forward to the chest while lowering the chin toward the knee.

c. Now lift and extend left thigh backward to a straight horizontal position, raising the head at the same time. Lower the left knee to the floor. Repeat with the right leg. Alternate this exercise three times with the left leg and then with the right leg; progress to ten repetitions on each side.

11. Rocking Chair

Objective: To stretch the hip, back, and shoulder muscles.

Exercise Progression:

a. Sit with the hands clasping the knees, pulling them toward the chest.

    b. Rock backward while exhaling forcefully.
    c. Continue rocking till resting on the upper back with the hips off the floor.
    d. Inhale and rock forward to the starting position. Continue motion. Start with five repetitions and eventually work up to ten.
12. Tail Wag
Objective: To relax muscle tension in the lower back.
Exercise Progression:
    a. Start in the "all fours" kneeling position, with elbows straight. Bend the head to the left to look over the left shoulder. Swing the pelvis to the left.
    b. Now swing the pelvis and head to the right. This action is similar to the way a dog wags its tail. Start with five to eight repetitions in each direction; progress to 15 repetitions.
13. Swing Back Stretcher
Objective: To strengthen and stretch the muscles of the arms, shoulders, and back.
Exercise Progression:
    a. Start in the "all fours" kneeling position, with elbows straight. Now lean forward over the hands, with elbows locked.
    b. Lean backward, placing buttocks on heels.
    c. Bend at the hips and lower head toward the floor, between arms, trying to touch forehead to knees. Keep the elbows straight, with only the hands touching the floor. Return to the starting position. Repeat the forward and backward swinging movements three times and progress to eight to ten repetitions.

Vigorous Standing Activities

These exercises are intended to:

- stretch and improve endurance of the abdominal, trunk, and lower back muscles

- improve the flexibility of the arm and shoulder muscles, particularly at the shoulder girdle and shoulder joints
- increase the endurance and range of motion of the buttock, anterior and posterior thigh, lower leg, and foot muscles
- improve cardiovascular fitness through performing exercise continuously for longer periods of time.

It is important to warm up for five to ten minutes with walking, chair-supported, or floor activities before moving on to these more vigorous exercises. Exhibit 6–4 is a summary listing of the vigorous standing activities.

1. Standing Knee Grabber
   Objective: To stretch the muscles of the back thighs and buttocks, as well as the muscles on the front of the thigh and hip.
   Exercise Progression:
   a. Stand erect, with legs together and arms at the sides.
   b. Raise the right knee with both hands and press it to the chest.
   c. Repeat with the left knee and return to the starting position. Alternate with each leg three times and progress to eight repetitions.

2. Windmill Arm Circles
   Objective: To loosen and flex the arms at the shoulders.
   Exercise Progression:
   a. Stand erect, with feet slightly apart and arms crossed in front of body.
   b. Make a large circle with the arms by lifting and swinging them out to the sides.
   c. Continue the arm movement upward, crossing the arms above the head before starting the downward motion.
   d. Finish the downward circling while crossing the arms in front of the body. Repeat the upward circling action. Now, with the arms above the head, make large downward circles. Repeat five times and progress to ten to fifteen repetitions in each direction.

Exhibit 6–4 Vigorous Standing Activities

Exercise Number	Title	Brief Description	Beginning Number of Repetitions
1.	Standing Knee Grabber	Alternate knee lift and squeeze to chest.	3, each leg
2.	Windmill Arm Circles	Circle extended arms in clockwise and counterclockwise directions in front of body.	5, each direction
3.	Trunk Bend and Stretcher	Alternate sideward bend to right and left with arm overhead.	5, each side
4.	Side Leg Lunge and Stretcher	Alternately bend to left bent knee position and then to right.	4, each side
5.	Trunk Twister	From erect hands-behind-head position, alternately twist right and left.	3, each direction
6.	Heel Raiser and In-Place Running	Lift heels and run in place for ten repetitions. Repeat cycle.	4 cycles
7.	Alternate Elbow to Knee Touch	From hands-behind-head position, twist and touch right elbow to lifted left knee. Alternate to lifted right knee.	4, each side
8.	Wing Stretcher	Swing elbows, then arms, backward from shoulder-level position.	4
9.	Iron Cross	Lift arms, swing back, then forward, from heel-lifted position.	3
10.	Arm Swinging Knee-Benders	Alternate arm swinging and knee bending with an easy bounce.	5–6 cycles

3. Trunk Bend and Stretcher
   Objective: To stretch the muscles on the side of the trunk and hips.
   Exercise Progression:
   a. Stand erect with feet 15 inches apart and both arms overhead.
   b. Bend the trunk to the right, dropping the right arm. Return to the starting position. Pause for three seconds before continuing.
   c. Now bend the trunk to the left, dropping the left arm. Return to the starting position. Repeat five times to the right and five times to the left, alternately. Progress to ten repetitions on each side.
4. Side Leg Lunge and Stretcher
   Objective: To stretch and strengthen the thigh and hip muscles.
   Exercise Progression:
   a. Stand erect, with feet three feet apart and arms at the sides.
   b. Bend and place the hands on the left knee, keeping the weight over the left foot. Keep the right foot flat on the floor and stretch the right thigh. Hold this position for three seconds and then return to the starting position. Repeat the same movements to the right side, holding for three seconds, and returning to the starting position.
   c. Repeat alternately three or four times to the left and right; progress to eight to ten repetitions on each side.
5. Trunk Twister
   Objective: To stretch and loosen the muscles of the trunk.
   Exercise Progression:
   a. Stand erect with hands interlocked firmly behind the neck.
   b. Twist the trunk as far as possible to the right without moving the feet and return to the starting position.
   c. Now twist the trunk to the left. Return to the starting position. Alternately repeat motion to the left and right two or three times and progress to ten repetitions.
6. Heel Raiser and In-Place Running
   Objective: To strengthen the calf and leg muscles and contribute to cardiorespiratory fitness.

Exercise Progression:
a. Stand erect with the arms to the sides. Rise on the toes. Lower the heels.
b. Now slowly run in place, stepping up and down ten times. Again rise on toes, hold for a three-second count, and lower the heels. Repeat this cycle three or four times and progress to ten repetitions.

7. Alternate Elbow to Knee Touch
   Objective: To stretch arm, shoulder, back, and trunk muscles and strengthen the hip and abdominal muscles.
   Exercise Progression:
   a. Stand erect, with hands interlocked firmly behind the neck.
   b. Twist the trunk to the right and bend to touch the right elbow to lifted left knee. Balance carefully on the standing foot.
   c. Repeat the same movements by turning the trunk to the left. Alternately repeat three or four elbow-to-knee touches to the right and to the left. Progress to ten repetitions on each side.

8. Wing Stretcher
   Objective: To stretch the muscles of the chest, shoulders, and upper arms, and strengthen the muscles of the upper back.
   Exercise Progression:
   a. Stand erect, with the arms at shoulder height in front of the body, palms down.
   b. Swing the elbows backward until the tips of the fingers are touching the midline of the chest.
   c. Press elbows farther back, at shoulder level.
   d. Extend the arms to the side, still at shoulder level. Return to the starting position. Repeat three or four times and progress to ten repetitions.

9. Iron Cross
   Objective: To stretch the muscles in the back of the legs and to tone the muscles of the upper arms, shoulders, and back.
   Exercise Progression:
   a. Stand erect, with feet together and arms at the sides.
   b. Lift the straight arm to shoulder height in front of the body while rising on the toes.

    c. Now swing the arms to the sides while remaining on the toes.

    d. Swing the arms back to the forward position, continuing to remain on toes.

    e. Lower the arms and heels to the starting position. Repeat two or three times. As balance and coordination improve, build up to six or seven repetitions.

10. Arm Swinging Knee-Benders

    Objective: To stretch the arms and shoulders and strengthen the front thigh and hip muscles.

    Exercise Progression:

    a. Stand erect, with the right arm forward and left arm extended backward.

    b. Now bend knees, in a dropping motion, while swinging the right arm backward and left arm forward.

    c. Straighten knees and dip again while swinging the right arm forward and the left arm backward in full swings. Repeat five or six of these arm-swinging and knee-bending "dipping" movements. Gradually build up to 15 or 20 repetitions.

NOTE

1. Arthur Steinhaus, personal communication.

Chapter 7

Walking: Oft Neglected Highly Recommended

Leonard Biegel

The wandering man knows of certain ancients, far gone in years, who have staved off infirmities and dissolution by earnest walking—hale fellows, close upon ninety, but brisk as boys.

Charles Dickens

Walking is probably the most popular form of exercise in the United States. The President's Council on Physical Fitness and Sports states that nearly 35 million adults walk for exercise virtually every day, and another 15 million do so two or three times a week. In fact, the council reports that in a recent national survey, the highest percentage of regular walkers (39.4 percent)[1] in any group was found among men 65 years of age and older. No evidence is presented, however, to indicate how many walk correctly or to the best advantage.

WALKING AS AEROBIC EXERCISE

Walking is an aerobic exercise (i.e., it improves the functioning of the body's oxygen-processing system). Walking gently strains the respiratory system, taxing the ability of the lungs to process a sufficient amount of oxygen into the blood stream and forcing the heart to pump harder to deliver more oxygen-carrying blood to the tissues. The same strain is placed on the arteries and capillaries, for they are being asked to provide more oxygen-filled blood to the cells. As a walking program progresses, the heart becomes stronger and better able to perform increased workloads.

WALKING AS A PRESCRIPTION FOR FITNESS

Walking is by no means a novel fitness prescription. Hippocrates, the father of modern medicine, was prescribing walking for his patients in 400 BC. He suggested an early morning walk for patients with mental problems and fast walking for weight loss.

Oliver Wendell Holmes wrote, in *The Autocrat of the Breakfast Table:*

> In walking, the will and muscles are so accustomed to work together and perform their task with so little expenditure of force, that the intellect is left comparatively free. The mental pleasure in walking, as such, is in the sense of power over all our moving machinery.[2]

People walk for many reasons: for pleasure, to rid themselves of tension, to find solitude, or just to get from one place to another. Nearly everyone who walks regularly does so—at least in part—because of a conviction that it is good exercise.

Often dismissed in the past as too easy, walking is gaining new respect as a means of improving physical fitness. When done briskly on a regular schedule, walking can improve the body's ability to utilize oxygen during exertion, lower the resting heart rate, reduce blood pressure, and increase the efficiency of the heart and lungs. It also helps burn calories. Since obesity and high blood pressure are among the leading risk factors for heart attack and stroke, walking offers some protection against two of our major killers.

Walking is not as efficient an exercise as running and other more strenuous activities, but the difference is not as great as many believe. Jogging a mile in 8½ minutes burns only 26 calories more than walking a mile in 12 minutes.

Walking can help you lose weight. On the average, a three-mile walk in an hour's time by a 160-pound person burns about 285 calories. The same activity by a person weighing 120 pounds would use about 215 calories. While this may not seem like much, 215 calories burned up four times a week can produce a 13-pound weight loss in a year without any reduction in the calories you consume.[3]

There is a difference between the aerobic advantages of strolling and walking. While strolling relieves tension and provides social and esthetic outlets, it cannot be classified as a fitness program; walking, on the other hand, can be. Before prescribing a walking methodology, it is important to understand the specific characteristics of walking as a fitness program.

CHARACTERISTICS OF A WALKING PROGRAM

Walking has actually proven to be more effective as a fitness program than running and other highly touted activities. Unlike other activities, walking is virtually injury-free, and it has the lowest dropout rate of any form of exercise. Here are some facts about walking:

- Because walking is more natural and less strenuous—and in fact, more interesting—than some other exercises, more people stay with the regimen over a longer period of time than with any other exercise. This is important, for fitness programs cannot work overnight. If the individual does not stay with the fitness program, it is quite easy to lapse back into the deconditioned state that preceded it.
- Walking appears to have a substantial psychological payoff. Beginning walkers almost invariably report that they feel better, sleep better, and that their mental outlook has improved.
- Aside from the sheer enjoyment of seeing places and people, arms and legs become stronger and more flexible, and, in general, the person moves about with greater ease.

- Smokers who begin walking often cut down or quit. There are two reasons: one, it is difficult to exercise vigorously if one also smokes, and two, better physical condition encourages a desire to improve other aspects of one's lifestyle.
- Almost everyone can do it—one does not need lessons to learn how to walk, and the rules of aerobic walking are simple.
- Walking can be done almost anywhere. A sidewalk, street, road, trail, park, field, or shopping mall will do. The variety of possible settings is one of the factors that makes walking a practical and pleasurable activity.
- Walking can be done almost anytime. There is no need to find a partner or get a team together, and except for rain or snow, walking can be enjoyed in all weather. (Many people have also found interesting indoor solutions to the inclement weather problem.)
- Walking is free: no one has to join a private club to become a walker. The only equipment required is a sturdy, comfortable pair of shoes with resilient heels.
- While running has certain advantages, it is not recommended for older people—particularly those who are beginners. Furthermore, running is more natural for thin-boned, muscular persons and less so for those who are heavier; walking does not produce the sudden strain on the heart that running does; and walking is easier on the joints and bones. Granted, walking takes longer than running to produce the same effects, but consider this: an hour of walking at 3¾ miles per hour burns 300 calories while benefiting the heart, lungs, vascular system, and muscles.
- Current data indicate that a good walking regimen can be just as beneficial as running. John T. Davis, in his book, *Walking!*, says:

Several researchers have commented on how walking compares to running in producing physical fitness. One of the primary ways physiologists determine if an exercise is resulting in greater cardiorespiratory fitness is by measuring the training heart rate. Everyone has a maximum heart rate, which is roughly 220 beats a minute minus your age. Physiologists consider it necessary to have a rate of around 60 percent of the maximum to produce a training effect or an improvement in physical fitness. In a study at Wake Forest University, Dr. Michael L. Pollock and other researchers found that some men who walked faster than four miles an hour had a training heart rate from 80 to 90 percent of their maximum. The researchers reported in the *Journal of Applied Physiology* that the results of the walking study compared favorably with eleven other studies conducted on men from forty to sixty years old who had been trained by running and swimming. As a matter of fact, the researchers found that the improvement in the subjects' physical fitness was three times as great as the improvement in some running programs. They also found that walking faster than four miles an hour burned up more calories than jogging at slower speeds.[4]

- Walking is good exercise for the legs, heart, and lungs, but it is not a complete exercise program. Thus, specific warm-up exercises are included later in this chapter.

GROUND RULES

Walking is possibly the most logical, universal exercise for older people. But like any other regimen, it has its ground rules.

According to Casey Conrad, executive director of the President's Council on Physical Fitness and Sports, "It's so simple I almost hate to explain how. The simple mechanics of walking are heel-to-toe (putting your heel down first and rocking to your toe) and not to toe out (pointing your toes outward). You must stretch and walk briskly. Most of the time the best way to learn walking is by walking." Conrad offers a slogan for walkers: "You can't walk away from your troubles, but you can sometimes walk them off."[5]

Warm-up and Cool-down Routines

Exercises for warming up and cooling down are strongly recommended, because walking, like any other exercise, tends to tighten muscles, tendons, and ligaments in the back of the legs. Strengthening exercises help keep the muscles flexible. The exercises that follow are designed to increase flexibility, strengthen muscles, and serve as a warm-up prior to walking:

- *Stretcher*. Stand facing a wall at arm's length, with back straight and heels firmly on the floor. Place the palms flat against the wall, slightly below shoulder height. Slowly bend the elbows until the forehead touches the wall. Tuck hips toward the wall and hold this position for 20 seconds. Repeat the exercise with knees slightly flexed.
- *Reach and Bend*. Stand erect, with feet 12 inches apart and arms extended over head. Reach as high as possible while keeping the heels on the floor and hold for ten seconds. Flex the knees slightly and bend slowly at the waist, touching the floor between the feet with the fingers. Hold for ten seconds. Repeat entire sequence two to five times.
- *Knee Pull*. Sit with legs extended. Lock the arms around both legs behind the knees and pull the knees to the chest, raising the buttocks slightly off the floor. Hold for 10 to 15 seconds. Repeat the exercise three to five times.
- *Sit-up*. Several versions of the sit-up are listed in order of difficulty, easiest one first, most difficult last. Start with the sit-up that can be done three times without undue strain. When ten repetitions can be done without great difficulty, progress to a more difficult version.

  1. Lie on the back with arms at sides, palms down, and knees slightly bent. Curl the head forward until you can see past feet, hold for three seconds, then slowly lower to the starting position. Repeat the exercise three to ten times.
  2. Lie flat on the back with arms at the sides, palms down, and knees slightly bent. Roll forward until the upper body is at a 45° angle to the floor, hold for three seconds, then return slowly to the starting position. Repeat the exercise three to ten times.
  3. Lie on the back with arms at the sides, palms down, and knees slightly bent. Roll forward to the sitting position, hold

for three seconds, then return slowly to the starting position. Repeat the exercise three to ten times.

4. Lie on the back with arms crossed on the chest and knees slightly bent. Roll forward to the sitting position, hold for three seconds, then return slowly to the starting position. Repeat the exercise three to ten times.

5. Lie on the back, with hands laced in back of the head and knees slightly bent. Roll forward to the sitting position, hold for three seconds, then return to the starting position. Repeat the exercise 3 to 15 times.

Checking Your Walking Form

The American Medical Association has outlined a method for checking one's walking form:

1. Stand eight to ten feet from a full-length mirror, with toes straight ahead and feet four inches apart.
2. Bend the right knee and swing the right leg forward from the hip.
3. Place the right heel on the floor as weight is pushed over the right foot. Keep the toes straight ahead.
4. Push the weight over the right foot by straightening the right knee and pushing off with the left toes. The body is leaning forward slightly. Do not push too forcefully or the trunk will fall forward.
5. Bend the left knee. Carry the left foot through and place the left heel on the floor.
6. Push the weight over the left foot by straightening the left knee and pushing off with the right toes. The body is leaning forward slightly.[6]

Correct walking is a combination of pushing the body forward and using the pull of gravity. A common fault is leaning forward too much, using gravity alone to regulate the gait; this results in a jarring walk. While walking toward the mirror, stop at various points to check details.

Consciously keep the weight from rolling to the inside of the feet as the back leg is carried forward—walking with feet turned out lacks grace.

Developing an Efficient Walking Style

What makes a walk a workout is largely a matter of pace and distance. When walking for exercise, don't saunter, stroll, or shuffle. Instead, move at a steady clip that is brisk enough to make the heart beat faster and cause deep breathing.

Some tips to help develop an efficient walking style:

- A good pair of shoes is the only special equipment needed. Any shoes that are comfortable, provide good support, and don't cause blisters or calluses will do, but here are some specific suggestions:

    1. Good running shoes (the models with heavy soles) are good walking shoes, as are some of the lighter trail and hiking boots and casual shoes with rubber soles.
    2. Whatever kind of shoe, it should have arch supports and should elevate the heel ½ to ¾ inch above the sole of the foot.
    3. Choose a shoe with uppers made of materials that "breathe," such as leather or nylon mesh.
    4. Don't wear new shoes on a long walk until they are broken in. This requires about two days of light wearing.
    5. Socks should be absorbent, comfortable, and of adequate length. While support socks are appropriate for people who stand still a great deal, they are not recommended for walking. Toenails should be trimmed straight across.

- Weather will dictate the rest of one's attire. As a general rule, wear somewhat lighter clothing than the temperature would otherwise indicate (walking generates body heat). In cold weather, it is better to wear several layers of light clothing than one heavy layer. The extra layers help trap heat, and they are easy to shed if it becomes too warm. A wool cap will also trap body heat and provide protection for the head in very cold temperatures. Regardless of the weather, clothing should be loose, allowing for free motion.

- Hold the head erect, keep the back straight, and the abdomen flat. Toes should point straight ahead and arms should swing loosely at the sides.
- To warm up, walk slowly for the first five minutes.
- Land on the heel and roll forward to drive off the ball of the foot. Walking only on the ball of the foot or in a flat-footed style causes fatigue and soreness.
- Breathe deeply with mouth open, if that is more comfortable.
- Take long, easy steps, approximately 28 inches or more, measured from the heel of the forward foot to the toe of the rear foot. Approximately 120 steps per minute is a comfortable pace. Walking 3 to 3½ miles per hour is not running, but it is faster than window-shopping. Don't strain for distance.
- The "talk test" can determine an appropriate pace. One should be able to carry on a conversation while walking. If the walker is too breathless to talk, the pace is too fast.
- Listen to the body when walking or doing any exercise. Dizziness, pain, nausea, or any other unusual symptom indicates the need to slow or stop. If the problem persists, a physician should be consulted before exercising again.
- Exercise duration should, ideally, be 45 minutes to one hour. Walking should be continuous; thus, when waiting for a traffic light to change, mark time in place, so that the buildup of breathing and heart rate is maintained throughout the walking session. Although speed is important, the first goal is to walk continuously. For many people, this will require gradual increases from day to day. Only after appropriate duration is established should speed be increased.
- Look for a variety of destinations, including those in different directions from home; special routes reached after a reasonable ride from home; and alternates during inclement weather, such as the long corridors of enclosed shopping malls or apartment corridors. Special routes or paths should be investigated in advance to avoid dangerous surprises. The popular Billy Goat Trail in Great Falls, Maryland, for example, sounds like a

pleasant trail along the Potomac. Indeed it begins that way, only to become a rocky, often precarious, precipice.

- When walking up or down hills, or at a very rapid pace, lean forward slightly.
- Compete with oneself when walking. Even individuals of similar age and build vary widely in capacity for exercise. The objective should be to steadily improve personal performance, not to walk farther or faster than someone else.
- Cooling down is important, helping the increased heart rate to slow gradually without shock. Again, for many people it is easiest simply to slow down for the last five minutes of the walk.
- Relax at the end of a walk in a warm, soapy bath and gently massage the feet. Once out of the bath, elevate the feet while resting.

Most important, set aside a part of the day—the same time each day—to walk.

Several organizations with local chapters throughout the country have organized walking programs appropriate for individuals or group referrals:

- The National Audubon Society
  8940 Jones Mill Road
  Chevy Chase, Maryland 20815
- The Sierra Club
  1050 Mills Tower
  270 Bush Street
  San Francisco, California 94104
- National Campers and Hikers Association
  7172 Transit Road
  Buffalo, New York 14221

Local Y's, park services, and city and county recreation departments also organize frequent walking tours. Their offerings are another way to diversify a daily walking regimen.

NOTES

1. President's Council on Physical Fitness and Sports, *Walking for Exercise and Pleasure* (Washington, D.C.: Government Printing Office, 1980).

2. Oliver Wendell Holmes, *The Autocrat of the Breakfast Table*. William Morrow and Co., 1977.

3. Jane E. Brody, *The New York Times*, May 28, 1980.

4. John T. Davis, *Walking!* (New York: Bantam Books, 1979).

5. Casey Conrad, personal communication.

6. *The ABC's of Perfect Posture*, American Medical Association, Chicago, Ill., Pamphlet.

Chapter 8

Dance/Movement Therapy

Susan L. Sandel and Maryellen Kelleher

In our mechanized society, with its emphasis on leisure time, people become less and less active with advancing age. This is often encouraged by well-meaning friends and relatives, who urge the elderly to take it easy and not to strain themselves when participating in sports or performing household chores. For those confined to a convalescent home these problems are intensified. There, the older person's role is typically that of a passive recipient of nursing care. Often the staff is too busy providing basic medical care to focus on the residents' other physical and psychosocial needs. An atmosphere in which motionlessness prevails is not unusual in many nursing homes. The severely restricted capabilities of the patients themselves and the confining nature of the institution tend to reinforce this inactivity.

INACTIVITY AND AGING

Many disabilities commonly associated with old age are accepted as an inevitable consequence of growing old. Recently, researchers and clinicians have begun to challenge this longstanding belief. They are learning that many of the health problems of older people are not the inevitable consequence of old age but the result of a sedentary life style.[1,2,3]

For example, one of the most common conditions of old age, arteriosclerosis, is characterized by accumulation of fatty deposits in the arteries of the heart, brain, extremities, and kidneys. Arteriosclerosis contributes to heart disease, stroke, walking disabilities, and poor organ function and accounts for approximately half of all deaths in the United States. Commonly thought to be an inevitable consequence of old age, arteriosclerosis is actually the result of decreased activity.[4] As one ages and becomes less active, muscle mass is replaced by fat tissue. Conversely, increasing the amount of muscle mass can help to counteract fatty tissue replacement; muscle mass can be increased, regardless of age, through physical activity.

Inactivity also contributes to a host of other symptoms associated with old age. Inactivity facilitates accumulation of free-floating tension, manifested in such symptoms as insomnia, irritableness, and restlessness.[5] This is especially so for those confined to bed or wheelchair, who get very little exercise. Restlessness and insomnia are often treated with drug therapy or physical restraint rather than with activities designed to reduce tension.

Depression is another condition prevalent among the institutionalized elderly. Loss of societal role, material deprivation, physical decline, or loss of a spouse can trigger depression. One of the prime signs of depression is inactivity. A vicious cycle can easily develop in which depression and inactivity reinforce each other, and it can become increasingly difficult for the individual to interrupt this debilitating pattern.

Physical activity stimulates functioning of the respiratory, circulatory, and skeletal systems. Exercise also promotes and maintains muscle tone, balance and coordination, and spatial orientation. The old adage, "use it or lose it," applies not only to physical vigor, but to memory, orientation, social skills, and the ability to give and receive affection.

TREATMENT MODALITIES

Movement is a part of many different treatment modalities for the aged. Physical therapy (including exercise programs) as well as creative movement and dance/movement therapy all utilize physical activity.

Fitness programs offer exercises of varying levels of difficulty, depending upon the stamina and overall health of the participants. Goals of such programs might include increased mobility, improved circulation and breathing, and relaxation and release of tension; emotional well-being is a byproduct of better physical functioning. Although exercise programs are usually performed in a group, the emphasis is on the individual's experience and improvement.

Dance Movement Therapy

Creative movement, as a therapy for the aged, has been widely used in nursing homes and senior centers recently. Goals of creative movement programs include the same ones that characterize fitness programs (with the additional aims of increasing self-esteem and social interaction).[6] Classes include a variety of movement activities, often accompanied by music, designed to encourage creativity, spontaneity, and bodily awareness within a social setting.

Dance/movement therapy integrates physiological, psychological, and sociological aspects and attempts to give meaning to movement through the development of images within the movement interaction. While encouraging emotional reactions and processing of affective responses (both positive and negative), dance/movement therapy also facilitates social interaction. Movement activities are not the goal of the group experience, but rather the tool for creating a therapeutic environment. This approach distinguishes dance/movement therapy from other physical movement therapies and offers a comprehensive treatment method for the elderly.

Dance/Movement Distinctions

The American Dance Therapy Association defines dance/movement therapy as "the psychotherapeutic use of movement as a process which furthers the emotional and physical integration of the individual."[7] It is distinguished from other uses of dance (i.e., purely social) by its focus on the nonverbal communicative aspects of behavior and the use of movement as the mode of intervention in the therapeutic relationship. Dance/movement therapy includes a variety of approaches in which the therapist and client use movement as a medium for communication.[8] Approaches usually do not rely on structured exercises but rather on the spontaneous unfolding of interaction among participants.

Presently, the terms "dance" and "movement" therapy are used interchangeably. Although the American Dance Therapy Association recognizes a Registered Dance Therapist as the qualified practitioner, "movement" is used by therapists who wish to convey a broader meaning to their work. Particularly in geriatric settings, the term movement therapy is more widely used because "dance" is easily misunderstood by people who feel that their physical capabilities are limited. Even the term movement therapy may require explanation, because it can be confused with physical or occupational therapy.

History of Dance/Movement Therapy

Dance/movement therapy was introduced into geriatric patient programs as early as 1942, when Marian Chace, a pioneer of group dance therapy for hospitalized psychiatric patients, began working with elderly patients at St. Elizabeth's Hospital in Washington, D.C. Since then, several therapists have been refining and adapting dance/movement therapy techniques for use with convalescent home patients.[9,10,11] The model program created by senior author Susan L. Sandel at the Sound View Specialized Care Center, West Haven, Connecticut, utilizes a group-oriented, interactional approach focusing on the psychosocial benefits to the participants. Action is a vehicle for interaction; physical movement is used to foster social interaction and expression of feelings. Patients also derive physiological benefits from the activity, including improvement in cognitive functioning, which, in turn, affects the ability to interact with others.

Dance/movement therapy seems to have the potential for reaching a wide range of people. Whereas other movement approaches may require task completion, exercise mastery, fine motor coordination, or mental alertness, dance/movement therapy in its most basic form requires participation on a sensory-motor level, thereby tapping into the natural response to rhythm and touch. Patients who might otherwise be excluded from activities can function in a dance/movement therapy group.

Dance/Movement Therapy Techniques

A typical session begins with the patients sitting in a circle (in many convalescent homes, the majority of patients are in wheelchairs). Basic warm-up exercises, which the patients themselves may direct, help to stimulate muscles and nerves. Music initially provides a rhythmic framework, although it need not be used for the entire session. The warm-up movements suggest images that may be related to past life experiences or current concerns. The images provide a focus for meaningful interaction among group members and often stimulate discussion. Sessions always end with a sound and movement ritual that has been created by the group.

Specific techniques that have proved most useful in the authors' model dance/movement therapy program include:

Circle Formation. The circle formation is the primary spatial structure for unison action. It contributes to the feeling of group unity and increases the opportunity for eye contact. Because the therapist and patients are visible to everyone, those with hearing difficulties may participate in group movements by following others. Patients with visual impairments may be seated next to the therapist or other patients, who can describe the activity to them. Although ambulatory participants may move into other spatial formations such as lines, spirals, or a scatter around the room, the circle is still desirable for beginning and ending groups. The circle is particularly desirable for physically disabled and disoriented patients, for it facilitates touch and communication.

Mutual Touch. Mutual touch (such as patting, holding hands, and massage) is an extremely important element of dance/movement therapy sessions. This type of touching differs from the passive touch that convalescent home patients experience when they are bathed, fed, and dressed. Instead of being the passive recipient of physical contact, patients are encouraged to reach out to others to hold hands or pat someone's shoulder. In order to promote an atmosphere of mutuality, the therapist does not manipulate patients' limbs when they are having difficulty performing the movements. The attitude that patients "participate at their own level" is consistent with a nonmanipulative approach.

Music. Music often provides a useful stimulus for beginning a session, because it taps into the natural inclination to respond to rhythm. Music with a clear rhythmic beat is the most useful kind for dance/movement therapy sessions. This can include older music (from the patients' past) or more current music. Music should be playing as the group warms up; however, when recorded or instrumental music interferes with patients making their own sounds, singing songs, or engaging in discussion, the music should be discontinued. The therapist, if seated near the phonograph or tape recorder controls, can fade the music in and out as desired.

Vocalization. Whenever possible, patients should make sounds while moving. Sounding, even a "hum" or an "ah," stimulates breathing, circulation, and central body involvement. This technique is particularly useful for stroke or severely disabled patients whose speech is impaired; they may participate in making group sounds even if they cannot form words or participate in a variety of actions. Any sound that a patient offers is accepted and incorporated into the group experience. As people become more comfortable with vocalization, the therapist might encourage sounds that are expressive of particular feelings by asking, "What kind of sounds do we make when we're happy? sad? angry?" This, in combination with movements, can increase the range of expressive and communicative behavior.

Props. Certain objects are particularly useful for stimulating activity and encouraging interaction among convalescent home patients. Some favorite props are foam "Nerf" balls, colored scarves, and various lengths of stretch material.* These objects may be used initially to motivate movements such as squeezing, punching, tugging, and throwing, which may develop into participatory games. Props may be used to provide increased sensory stimulation and to link group members together to increase interpersonal awareness.

In one session, people took turns pulling on a long cloth rope. I suggested a tug of war with a partner, subsequently suggest-

---

*A comprehensive list of props may be found in Lindner et al., *Therapeutic Dance/Movement for Older Adults* (New York: Human Sciences Press, 1979).

ing they add the words, "give it to me." Several participants became engaged in vigorous struggles for the rope.

I then asked the participants if they fight for things they want nowadays. One man answered, "My place is on the sunporch. I don't want people around. I don't want to talk, just dream." A woman answered, "What's there to fight for? There's no point." The imagery facilitated a group discussion about whether there are still things worth fighting for in life. Several people were surprised when others expressed opinions or interests similar to their own.[12]

In groups with disoriented or confused patients, props may be the external focus or support that keeps the group together. In sessions with more alert patients, props may serve as the initial stimuli for interaction but may not be necessary later on (as group members begin to interact freely with one another).

Empathic Movement. One of the major distinguishing characteristics of dance/movement therapy from other body disciplines is the therapist's reliance on empathic movement as the basis for group interaction. Developed by pioneer dance therapist Marian Chace, empathic movement is a technique in which the therapist guides and develops group interaction as it unfolds during the session. Most dance/movement therapists who use this technique do not come to a session with a preconceived plan of activities but rely on verbal and nonverbal cues from the participants, coupled with their own intuitive responses, for the contents of the session. Suggestions, rather than commands, characterize this approach, so that the therapist is cast in the role of catalyst, not teacher.

When using the empathic movement approach, the therapist first creates an atmosphere that encourages self-expression through movement. The dance/movement therapist then responds to the feelings and thoughts being expressed, rather than imposing specific muscle movements to condition postural changes or evoke certain emotions.[13] This technique challenges the therapist's skill in dealing with spontaneous movement expressions and group process.

Imagery. The development of group images is another technique of dance/movement therapy distinguishing it from other physical movement therapies. The use of imagery shifts the experience from that of a simple action to a symbolic, shared act. A basic guideline for this technique is to begin with the movement and allow the image to develop from the action. For example, if the group movement involves stamping feet, the therapist might ask, "What can we stamp on?" or "Have you ever stamped on something?" This approach encourages participants to express ideas and associations without binding the group to the therapist's own imagination.

Imagery can be useful in identifying feelings, relating movements to real situations, and facilitating reminiscing; thus, the developing of images gives meaning to the movements. Many patients in convalescent homes are not motivated to exercise for the physical benefits they might derive. The use of group images switches the focus from the action to the feelings, thoughts, and memories being expressed; this provides the motivation for movement.

Reminiscing. Dance/movement therapy sessions with the elderly provide an opportunity for reminiscing in a social context. Reminiscing by the aged can be an adaptive behavior and should be encouraged in the appropriate circumstances.[14,15,16] In group dance/movement therapy, reminiscing may aid in developing interaction among the participants. For example, rhythmic actions done in unison can uncover forgotten memories and feelings. These memories may be pleasant or painful or of past mastery experiences.

> In one group in a nursing home, the participants were all stretching their arms toward the center of the circle and pulling them back to their chests repeatedly. I asked, "What could we pull?" One client answered, "A rope on a boat." As we continued, moving together, I asked if anyone in the group had ever been on a boat. Several people replied affirmatively and a group discussion followed about the various boating and canoeing excursions that people had enjoyed as long ago as seventy years.[17]

The same guideline that applies to introducing imagery applies here: always begin with the movement and allow the image (and/or reminiscence) to develop from the action. Progression from the sensory experience (movement) to a symbolic one (image or association) permits spontaneous unfolding of material during the session. The therapist need not introduce a topic for the group arbitrarily, but can pick on the issue or concern suggested by the actual movements and images.

Benefits to Different Patients

The various goals of dance/movement therapy are appropriate for the needs of most convalescent home patients. Increasing activity, bridging isolation, and encouraging emotional expression and socialization can be helpful to all institutionalized people. Different types of patients within the convalescent home, however, have specific needs, which require variations in therapists' techniques.

Cognitively Impaired. People who suffer from recent memory loss, disorientation, confusion, and other signs of organic brain syndrome can benefit from a consistent and predictable group experience. Consistency in time, place, leadership, and activities helps patients remember or relate to aspects of the group. For example, one very confused woman does not remember the dance/movement therapy session outside of the room where it takes place. Once she enters the room, she knows what to expect and often begins doing warm-up exercises.

Reality orientation techniques may easily be incorporated into the dance/movement therapy session and can be included in the opening and closing rituals. A favorite activity in one of our groups is passing a foam ball and asking participants to say their name when they have the ball. This kind of structured interaction is reassuring when it happens at the beginning of each group; the activity itself becomes an orienting factor for the participants.

When participating in movements that recall past mastery experiences, confused patients often appear more alert and organized. Reminiscing often seems to stimulate immediate, if short-lived, cognitive reorganization.

One day as I was walking down the hallway gathering people for a group, I heard Ms. B's perseverative wails several doors from her room. The nurse's aide who was attempting to quiet her was relieved when I wheeled Ms. B. to the small room where the group meets. Gradually Ms. B. stopped her wailing, slumped down in her chair, and lapsed into an apparent stupor. "Well," I thought, "at least she's not screaming. Perhaps she feels comfortable here." As group members began their warm-up exercises, which led to reminiscing and conversation, Ms. B. remained unresponsive. Then Mr. J. initiated some vigorous swinging arm movements and bell-like sounds. Soon everyone (except Ms. B.) was swinging their arms rhythmically, chanting "bong, bong, bong." Suddenly Ms. B. lifted her head, opened her eyes, and said, "Big Ben." For several minutes she talked lucidly about her travels to London and responded to questions from others. Then her eyes closed and she again lapsed into her sleep-like state for the remainder of the group session.[18]

This kind of experience can change the group's perception of individuals, making it possible to tolerate periodic lapses in their participation or attention.

Physical actions that evoke images of concrete activities such as rowing a boat, washing clothes, or kneading dough usually reawaken memories of past experiences. These provide an excellent vehicle for discussion and sharing even among very confused people.

Direct physical contact also has a dramatic organizing effect on patients who drift in and out of reality. Sometimes people who usually appear disoriented can carry on a lucid conversation when they are holding hands with another person. Movement experiences involving physical contact (holding hands and swaying from side to side or patting other people's hands or faces, for example) are extremely effective in engaging confused patients.

Physically Disabled. Many nursing home patients have severely disabling conditions such as strokes, arthritis, or other degenerative illnesses. Physical limitations need not prevent patients from participating in movement therapy. An accepting, nonjudgmental atmosphere in which people feel free to function within the limits of their own capabilities is most useful for patients with severe physical handicaps. When the focus is on the psychosocial values of the group, rather than on the activity, even the most physically disabled persons can feel that they have something to offer. In such an environment, activities such as making sounds, singing, telling stories, or simply touching one another are especially important. In one group at the Sound View Specialized Care Center, a woman who is paralyzed on one side said, "We get together to be together. Then we do as much as we can do. It's okay."

A critical factor in creating an accepting atmosphere is the language that the therapist uses in guiding the group. For example, if the therapist were to say, "Everyone lift your right arm; now your left arm; now both arms," there might be several people who could not successfully do at least one of those activities. A person who feels obliged to do everything, in order to participate in the group, will probably drop out or otherwise resist. If directions are offered as *suggestions*, in a non-authoritarian style, it is less likely that people will feel excluded. For example, the therapist might say, "Can we lift one arm? How about the other arm? If you can only lift one arm, that's okay. Can anyone lift both arms? If not, lift one arm as high as you can. If you can't lift your arms, how about your fingers?" This approach makes it possible for participants to say, "No, I can't do this, but I can do . . ." As group norms develop, the patients themselves might come up with suggestions for including someone with a specific physical limitation.

Implicit in dance/movement therapy is the expectation that participants will attempt to move—an expectation that stimulates patients' feelings about their bodies and their physical limitations. The authors have observed that sometimes patients feel stupid or humiliated when they cannot do a movement "well." By creating a safe environment and not avoiding patients' difficulties, the therapist learns to tolerate patients' feelings about their disabilities, thus establishing a model for the group; people subsequently begin to talk about their limitations and be more supportive toward one another.

Emotionally Disturbed. More and more nursing homes are receiving patients diagnosed as psychologically disturbed. This is due partially to deinstitutionalization trends, which are emptying large state mental hospitals, and partially to physicians and families who are becoming increasingly aware of emotional disturbances in older people. Significant differences exist between the elderly person who is clinically depressed because of the sudden onset of a traumatic illness or the loss of a spouse and the older person with a long history of psychiatric disturbance. In the former case, the dance/movement therapy group can provide an opportunity for the patient to mobilize feelings of anger and frustration, express them through acceptable group activities, and gain support and validation through the sharing of these feelings. In the latter case, a person with chronic psychological problems can benefit from a dance/movement therapy program that offers a consistent, orienting environment within a social atmosphere.

Patients with longstanding emotional disturbances are often receiving antipsychotic or antidepressant medications. Proper medication management—combined with a structured interpersonal environment—often helps such patients maintain adaptive functioning and prevents further social withdrawal and regression. Dance/movement therapy has traditionally proven to be effective treatment for long-term psychiatric patients because of the opportunities it affords for unison rhythmic movement, channeled expressions of emotions, and socialization.[19,20]

Mentally Alert. Many residents of nursing homes are mentally alert but require nursing care for physical illnesses or injuries. Some do not require total care but live in an intermediate care facility or a skilled nursing facility because they are unable to find other suitable living arrangements. Often the traditional passive entertainment and recreational activities do not adequately stimulate the mentally alert person struggling to maintain functioning. Dance/movement therapy sessions that activate the body and mind through creative and expressive involvement can provide the necessary stimulation. Approaches that encourage patient autonomy and leadership are especially appropriate for such people (e.g., helping one another get to the group, taking turns leading exercises, choosing a name for the group, and involvement in group decision-making).

After patients learn a repertoire of movements, they can exert more leadership in the group's activities. The therapist, by assuming a nondirective but warm stance, becomes a resource person for the group rather than the sole authority. The therapist may suggest new movements or creative activities but should be responsive to patients' offerings, both verbal and nonverbal. In dance/movement therapy sessions with very alert people, movement images often stimulate lengthy discussions about the past and/or present. There may be just as much talking as there is moving in such groups; this is to be expected (and even encouraged).

Contraindications

Although most people confined to a convalescent home could derive mental and physical benefits from dance/movement therapy, not all are willing or able to participate in a group experience. Some patients who are not clinically depressed and who have many visitors and adequate family support build a life for themselves in the institution within their own rooms. They are reluctant to attend most recreational or therapeutic activities yet do not appear withdrawn or isolated. Staff generally hesitate to interfere with their routine because they appear content and do not present a management problem. Such patients could benefit from an individualized exercise program to prevent muscle atrophy and maintain mobility.

Another class of patients who may not be able to benefit from group dance/movement therapy are those with paranoia. Such patients usually exhibit suspicious and guarded behavior and require very structured environments. They may be upset by imagery or expressions of emotion and may become more paranoid in a group. Sometimes very elderly people use guarded behavior as a defense against fears about their declining mental and/or physical health; attempts to disrupt their routine or involve them in new activities may be disorienting. Such patients might be able to benefit from individually administered exercise programs if the reasons for treatment were clearly communicated.

Motivation

Programs that focus exclusively on physical exercise tend to fail when presented to convalescent home patients if the exercise has no meaning for the patients and thus offers little to motivate them to activity. Many people in this situation have no motivation to improve their range of motion, stamina, breathing, or flexibility. Comments such as "We're too old to do this" or "I've exercised enough in my lifetime" are common. A rationale for activity based solely on its physiological benefits is quickly rejected by those who no longer believe that their physical health will improve.

A strong group identity—with an emphasis on addressing interpersonal needs—is a motivating factor for attending dance/movement therapy sessions. The notion that "we are a group" is a powerful force in helping people get to the sessions even when they are not feeling particularly well. Once patients enter the room, see each other, perhaps hear music, it is difficult to resist involvement.

Motivation is an issue not only for the patients but also for the therapist who works in long-term care facilities. It is one thing to work at a senior center or adult education program with 50- or 60-year-olds who might prolong their independence through movement and creative expression therapy. It is quite another experience to sit in a room with 75- to 100-year-olds who can't see, hear, or speak intelligibly. In order not to be overwhelmed by feelings of pessimism and despair, it is essential in such a situation for the therapist to abandon traditional notions of cure. With rare exceptions, people are not going to get better. Often the therapist's role is not to promote cure by usual standards but to facilitate a supportive, humanizing environment in which people can express and share their fears, pleasures, and memories. Dance/movement therapy cannot cure paralysis or blindness, but it can provide a bridge for the isolation that people experience as a result of such limitations.

Establishing a Program

Until recently, there has been little demand for dance/movement therapy programs in convalescent homes. In both private and nonprofit facilities, priority has been given to providing basic medical services. The combination of (1) public consciousness-raising regarding institutional care of the elderly, (2) recent legislation concerning quality of treatment in long-term care facilities, and (3) increasing interest in the relationship between activity and health has evoked great interest in movement therapy for the elderly.

Administrative Support. Adequate administrative support is essential for the success of any new program. Administrative support can be clearly demonstrated by the hiring of qualified personnel at appropriate salaries, the acquisition of adequate supplies, and the allocation of suitable space. This will concretely demonstrate to staff, patients, and families, perhaps more effectively than any rhetoric, the administration's support of the dance/movement therapy program.

The administrator should differentiate the dance/movement therapy program from other recreational and leisure activities. Although these other activities are very important in the lives of many institutionalized patients, attendance is voluntary and may be sporadic. Dance/movement therapy sessions can be viewed as part of the patient's treatment and should be presented accordingly. The staff's attitude toward the sessions influences the patients' own attitudes; if the staff considers the sessions valuable, patients are more likely to attend.

Nursing Involvement. Nursing staff cooperation is absolutely essential to the survival of any program in a convalescent facility. Nursing personnel are responsible for the minute-to-minute care and management of all patients. They, to a great extent, control whether or not someone is dressed and ready to participate in therapeutic programs. Therefore, the therapist should encourage nursing staff involvement in the dance/movement therapy sessions. Ideally, all participating staff should attend sessions regularly; however, changes in the nursing staffs' schedules are common and often make regular attendance difficult. Whenever possible, a nurse or nurse's aide should attend sessions and be encouraged to pass on any observations to other nursing staff. If nursing personnel can participate regularly, they should be invited to do so.

The dance/movement therapist must spend time with the nursing staff, in in-service programs and informal exchanges of patient data. If occasionally a patient is not ready for a session, the therapist should find out why but be sympathetic to nursing personnel's stresses. Posting a list of the dance/movement therapy groups at each nurse's station, including the day, time, place, and participants facilitates cooperation.

Personnel. Dance/movement therapy sessions should be conducted by a qualified therapist. Ideally, an assistant should participate regularly in each group, especially in groups with confused or physically disabled people. In addition to providing logistical support (transporting patients, setting up the room, etc.), a co-leader or assistant can facilitate contact with patients who have difficulty participating. Any motivated staff members or students can assist in these groups if they (1) are able to attend regularly; (2) are receptive to supervision and guidance from the dance therapist; and (3) feel comfortable moving and enjoy spontaneous interaction with patients.

At the Sound View Specialized Care Center, for example, the therapeutic recreation director, physical therapists, social workers, and college students have, at various times, assisted in the dance/movement therapy groups. In-service training and staff meetings after each session clarify the assistants' role and provide an opportunity for teaching new skills.

Size of Groups. The potential for therapeutic benefit is maximized in groups of 8 to 12 people. Certainly, creative movement activities can be beneficial to patients in large group settings; small groups, however, are more conducive to reminiscing, self-disclosure, and sharing. A comprehensive group program in a convalescent home should offer both small and large group experiences as they provide very different social environments.

Referral Criteria. Referral criteria based on cognitive functioning seem to be more important than those based on physical capabilities. For example, it is possible to have ambulatory and nonambulatory patients in the same dance/movement therapy group, but very alert people are often intolerant of confused people. In a group of less mentally alert patients, it is helpful to have people at varying levels of confusion and responsiveness. If a group comprises only extremely withdrawn, non-verbal, or nonresponsive members, the therapist will work hard, see no results, and eventually feel quite frustrated. If, however, a few people—who, despite moderate confusion—can respond to music or touch, their energy will help others become involved. In a sense, patients act as catalysts or co-therapists by creating multiple lines of communication with other patients.

Space. A private, uncluttered room that can accommodate 12 to 15 chairs and/or wheelchairs is preferable for dance/movement therapy sessions. Recreational movement activities are often held in open lounges, but small groups are best conducted in a more protected space. This creates a safe atmosphere in which people feel free to express themselves.

CONCLUSION

An interactional approach to dance/movement therapy with the elderly can facilitate emotional expression, spontaneity, and peer interaction as well as increased bodily awareness and range of movement. Socialization is a primary goal of group approaches with convalescent home patients, along with the expression of feelings and the development of independent behavior. The isolation so prevalent in institutional settings can be alleviated by participation in group rhythmic movement activities, which lead to the sharing of feelings and memories.

Therapy facilitates recall of feelings and memories through involvement at the body level. When practiced within a setting in which group interaction and cohesion are fostered, it can provide an arena for very elderly people to express themselves and engage in social relationships. In addition to the obvious physical advantages of a regular program of activity, the psychosocial approach to dance/movement therapy offers a wide range of emotional and social benefits.

NOTES

1. W. Bortz, "Effect of Exercise on Aging—Effect of Aging on Exercise," *American Geriatrics Society* 28, no. 2 (1981): 49–51.

2. H. deVries, "Education for Physical Fitness in the Later Years," in *Learning for Aging*, ed. S. Grabowski and W. Mason (Washington, D.C.: Adult Education Association, 1974).

3. H. Kraus, *Principles and Practice of Therapeutic Exercise* (Springfield, Ill.: Charles C Thomas, 1956).

4. R. Keelor, "The Role of Physical Fitness in Reducing Health and Long-Term Care of the Elderly." Testimony to the joint hearing held by Subcommittees on Health and Long-Term Care, Federal, State and Community Relations, Select Committee on Aging, April 14, 1976.

5. L. Gulton, *Don't Give Up on an Aging Patient* (New York: Crown Publishing, 1975).

6. G. Herman and J. Renzurri, *Creative Movement for Older People* (Hartford, Conn.: Institute for Movement Exploration, 1978).

7. American Dance Therapy Association.

8. S. Chaiklin and C. Schmais, *American Handbook of Psychiatry*, ed. S. Arieti (New York: Basic Books, 1975), Chapter 37.

9. A. Samuels, "Dance Therapy for Geriatric Patients." Proceedings of the Eighth Annual Conference of the American Dance Therapy Association, 1973, pp. 27–30.

10. E.D. Garnet, "Geriatric Calisthenics: A Group Therapy Approach," *Writings on Body Movement and Communication*, Monograph 2 (American Dance Therapy Association, 1972).

11. I. Fersh, "Dance/Movement Therapy: A Holistic Approach to Working with the Elderly," *American Journal of Dance Therapy* 3, no. 2 (1980): 33–43.

12. S. Sandel, "Movement Therapy with Geriatric Patients in a Convalescent Home," *Hospital & Community Psychiatry* 29 (1978): 738–741.

13. M. Chace, *Marian Chace: Her Papers,* ed. H. Chaiklin (Columbia, Md.: American Dance Therapy Association, 1975).

14. R. Butler, "The Life Review: An Interpretation of Reminiscence in the Aged," *Psychiatry* 26 (1963): 65–75.

15. A.W. McMahon and P.J. Rhudick, "Reminiscing in the Aged: An Adaptational Response," in *Psychodynamic Studies on Aging,* ed. S. Sevin and R. Kahana (New York: International Universities Press, 1967).

16. R.D. Fallot, "The Life Story through Reminiscence in Later Adulthood" (Ph.D. diss., Yale University, 1967).

17. Sandel, "Movement Therapy."

18. S. Sandel, "Innovations in Psycho-Social Programming with the Aged," opening remarks at a conference, Connecticut Valley Hospital, Middletown, Conn., 1980.

19. S. Chaiklin and C. Schmais, "Chace Approach to Dance Therapy," in *Eight Theoretical Approaches in Dance-Movement Therapy,* ed. P.L. Bernstein (Iowa: Kendall/Hunt, 1979).

20. S. Sandel, *Dance Therapy for Geriatric Patients,* Proceedings of the Eighth Annual Conference of the American Dance Therapy Association, 1973, pp. 27–30.

Chapter 9

In the Swim

Leonard Biegel

INTRODUCTION

Swimming is a nearly perfect exercise, especially for older people. It is an activity that may be used for recreation on one day; physical conditioning on the next; and survival on another. Vigorous water activities can make a major contribution to flexibility, strength, and cardiovascular endurance. With the body submerged in water, water pressure increases blood circulation (to a degree) and helps promote deeper ventilation of the lungs.

Increased flexibility occurs in water because of the lessening of gravitational pull. A person immersed to the neck experiences an apparent 90 percent weight loss. Thus, a 130-lb. woman, when immersed in water, has only to support a weight of 13 lb. Older people with painful arthritic joints and weak leg muscles and those requiring reconditioning of the heart muscle will usually find it more comfortable to move in the water than on the floor. Many individuals who can do leg "bobbing" or jogging in the water could never do so on land.

SWIMMING PROGRAM ATTRIBUTES

Specific attributes of a swimming program include:

- All major muscle groups, including those of the arms, legs, and trunk, are exercised.

- Swimming strokes can be varied, so swimming is less tedious than some other regimens.
- Swimming has particular advantages for strengthening the back and abdominal muscles.
- For arthritics, swimming is important therapy. Water buoyancy permits the arthritic patient to move without putting unnecessary stress on the joints.
- Swimming may help to counter varicose veins. For the circulatory system in general, reasonably vigorous swimming, 20 to 30 minutes a day, three times a week provides aerobic conditioning comparable to jogging or brisk walking. (Fast swimming burns approximately 350 to 420 calories an hour.)
- Swimming is beneficial in combination with calisthenics and walking programs.
- Overweight people are very buoyant in water and thus find that swimming is easier than land exercises.

Swimming pool access is a major obstacle for many people. For those who live in colder climates, summer swimming is a seasonal novelty, with little lasting effect.

Professionals working with older people should seek year-round access to swimming pools at Y's, community centers, clubs, and schools. The most unexpected facility might become available at specific regular times for the modest collective fee an older group could offer.

Group and private lessons are available in virtually every community, with Y's offering probably the most extensive programs. Local universities and county and municipal recreation departments also offer programs in swimming instruction.

CAUTIONARY NOTES

Several cautionary notes are important:

- Cold water tends to stiffen muscles by restricting peripheral circulation and should be avoided. Heated pools, whether indoor or outdoor, are best. Warm lakes are frequently good, but ocean swimming should be avoided by those not physically fit because of the cold water and frequently unpredictable undercurrents.

- Qualified instructors should teach groups and individuals.
- A lifeguard should always be present; above all, one should never swim alone.
- Sore muscles can be avoided with warm-up exercises, beginning with a few minutes and eventually building up to a full 20- or 30-minute warm-up program.
- "Swimmer's ear," the common malady characterized by retention of water in the ear canal, can be prevented by making sure that trapped water is removed from the ear promptly. Many people shake the head vigorously or hop with the head tilted to one side while sealing the ear with a finger; others wear ear plugs. If symptoms such as itching or pain develop, see a physician promptly.
- Proper fitting goggles eliminate much of the irritation experienced because of chlorinated water; they also allow enjoyment of the underwater visual sensation: Some will gain water confidence from wearing goggles. Goggles should be adjusted to a proper fit; the elastic strap should be worn fairly high on the head to seal off the water.
- Cramps in the legs or feet develop if one overexerts, swims in cold water, or fails to do warm-up exercises. Knead a cramped spot with the thumbs, alternating with leg extensions.
- Never swim when very tired or after consuming a substantial meal or alcoholic drinks.

EXERCISES FOR SWIMMING

The exercises presented here, recommended as an auxiliary to lap swimming, have been prepared by the President's Council on Physical Fitness and Sports.[1] They are intended to provide a range of choices from which to create a particular day's or week's workout.

The Warm-up

Light conditioning and stretching exercises should be performed outside the pool before more vigorous activities are attempted. Participants should begin with light rhythmical work at a slow pace, accelerating the tempo gradually, alternating slow with faster work, until nearing perspiration.

Most swimming activities hyperextend the back; thus, specific back stretching exercises should be performed both at the beginning and end of the workout. For maximum benefit, stand erect with legs apart, extending the hands high overhead and reaching as high as possible. After approximately 5 to 10 seconds in the arms-overhead reaching position, bend the trunk forward, flexing the knees. Hold the bent-stretched position for approximately 20 to 30 seconds, then repeat the exercise.

Warm-up exercises raise the deep muscle temperature and stretch ligaments and connecting tissues, thus preparing the body for vigorous work and helping to avoid injury and discomfort.

Standing Water Drills

Performed while standing in waist-to-chest–deep water.

- Alternate Toe Touch
  1. Raise the left leg, bringing the right hand toward the left foot while looking back and extending the left hand rearward.
  2. Recover to starting position.
  3. Reverse.
- Side Straddle Hop
  With hands on hips:
  1. Jump sideward, to position the feet approximately 24 inches apart.
  2. Recover.
- Stride Hop
  With hands on hips:

1. Jump, with left leg forward and right leg back.
2. Jump, changing to right leg forward and left leg back as you move.

- Toe Bounce
  With hands on hips:
  1. Jump high, with feet together, through a bouncing movement of the feet.

- Toe Raise
  1. Rise on toes.
  2. Lower to starting position.
  3. Accelerate.

- Side Bender
  With left arm at side and right arm overhead:
  1. Stretch, slowly bending to the left.
  2. Recover to the starting position.
  3. Reverse.

- Standing Crawl
  Simulate the overhand crawl stroke by:
  1. Reaching with the left hand into the water, pressing downward, and pulling, bringing the left hand through to thigh.
  2. Repeat with right hand.

- Walking Twists
  With fingers laced behind neck:
  1. Walk forward, bringing up alternate legs, twisting the trunk to touch the knee with the opposite elbow.

- Bouncing
  1. Bounce on the left foot while pushing vigorously with both hands, causing the upper body to rise.
  2. Reverse.

- Jogging in Place
  Standing with arms bent in the running position:
  1. Jog in place.

- Bounding in Place with Alternate Arm Stretched Forward
  1. Bound in place with high knee action, right arm stretched forward when left knee is high, and the left arm stretched rearward.

2. Reverse.
Note: When the position of the arms and hands are reversed, one should pull down and through with hand, simulating a crawl stroke.

Pool-Side Standing Drills

Performed while standing adjacent to the pool wall, in mid-chest–deep water.

- Stretch and Touch
  Face the wall with shoulders under water, arms extended, and fingertips approximately 12 inches from the wall:
  1. Twist left and try to touch the wall with both hands.
  2. Reverse.
- Flat Back
  1. Press against the wall, holding for six seconds.
  2. Relax to the starting position.
- Leg out
  Stand with the back against the wall:
  1. Raise left knee to the chest.
  2. Extend the left leg.
  3. Stretch the left leg.
  4. Relax to the starting position.
  5. Reverse.

Edge-Holding Drills (Supine)

- Pool-Side Knees up
  Lying, with the back toward the pool wall, legs extended, holding on to the pool gutter with the hands:
  1. Bring knees to the chin.
  2. Relax to the starting position.
- Twisting Legs
  1. Twist slowly to the left.

2. Recover.
3. Reverse.

Edge-Holding Drills (Standing)

- Twist Hips
    1. Twist hips to the left as far as possible, keeping the trunk facing forward.
    2. Recover.
    3. Reverse.
- Alternate Raised Knee Crossovers
    1. Lift left knee.
    2. Cross over right leg.
    3. Twist to the right.
    4. Recover.
    5. Reverse.

Edge-Holding Drills (Prone)

- Legs Together
    1. Spread legs as far as possible.
    2. Pull legs vigorously together.
- Front Flutter Kicking
    1. Kick, flutter style (toes pointed back, ankles flexible, knees loose but straight, with the whole leg acting as a whip).

Treading Water

Performed in water deep enough so that toes will not touch bottom:

- Elementary Treading
    1. Scull or fin while kicking bicycle, scissors, or frog style.

- Advanced Treading
  1. Kick bicycle, scissors, or frog style, with arms held shoulder high.
- One-Hand–High Treading
  1. Kick bicycle, scissors, or frog style, holding one arm straight up, the other shoulder high.
  2. Reverse arm positions.
- Two-Hands–High Treading
  1. Kick bicycle, scissors, or frog style, holding both arms straight up out of the water.

Sculling

In several of the exercises, the term "sculling" is used. Sculling is a paddle-like motion of the arms and hands, usually begun by pushing the palm down with the arms at the sides. Hands are held flat, fingers together, thumbs close to the fingers. With thumbs up, one rotates the wrists, bringing the palms forward, then turning the palms downward and backward. The downward pressure should be held constant during sideward and forward movements. Lifting power is thus provided as the hands are drawn to the front and side, parallel to the water surface. Controlled breathing is essential. The swimmer should inhale through the mouth and exhale through the nose (exhale whenever the head is underwater).

Extension Exercises

- Left Knee up, Back
  From a prone position:
  1. Scull, drawing the left knee up to the chest, with the right leg extended and right toes out of the water.
  2. Scull, straightening the left leg and returning to the starting position.
  3. Reverse.

- Front and Back
  From a vertical position:
  1. Scull, drawing the knees to the chest, thrusting the legs forward to a back lying position.
  2. Scull, drawing the knees to the chest, thrusting the legs backward to a front lying (prone) position.
- Reverse Sides Extension
  From a vertical position:
  1. Scull, drawing the knees to the chest, and thrust the legs to the left, shifting the body to a right sidestroke position.
  2. Scull vigorously, drawing the knees to the chest, and thrust the legs to the right, shifting body to a left sidestroke position.

Other Water Exercises

- Alternate Sculling and Treading
  From a vertical position:
  1. Tread water with the arms held shoulder high.
  2. Shift to sculling action, with the knees bent so that the heels are under the hips. Scull without the use of the legs for a specified time (approximately ten seconds).
- Sculling "V" Sit
  From a supine position:
  1. Lower the hips and raise the feet out of the water, with the toes pointed, so that the body is in a "V" position.
  2. Scull forward for a specified time (approximately ten seconds).

Lap Swimming

Despite the small distance covered in the average residential pool after pushing off the pool-side and gliding, lap swimming is still excellent exercise. If the pool is uncrowded, the swimmer should swim hard until beginning to feel winded, then swim more lazily, with a breast or side stroke, until recovered. Another way to begin an interval training program is to swim one pool length, get out, walk to the starting point, and repeat a number of times. For an individual in poor physical condition, a regimen of five to ten lengths, walking back after each length, may be necessary for several weeks or months; as endurance improves the number of lengths can be increased progressively.

NOTE

1. President's Council on Physical Fitness and Sports, *Physical Fitness Research Digest*.

Chapter 10

Arthritis and Exercise

Carole Lewis

During a lifetime, the musculoskeletal system undergoes a great deal of use, misuse, neglect, and trauma. These factors promote arthritic changes. Osteoarthritis affects half of the population in their 50s and 85 percent of those in their 70s.[1] Therefore, when designing an exercise program for the elderly, the effects of joint trauma must be considered. Elements such as when, where, why, and how to exercise should be understood. Since pain is an integral part of arthritis, ways of working with pain should be explored. Understanding the facts can promote optimum exercise benefits for the older person with arthritis.

WHAT IS ARTHRITIS?

Arthritis literally means joint (arthr) inflammation (itis). The term, however, has become an umbrella for very diverse types of joint and secondary muscular disease. The following are brief descriptions of some of the more prevalent types of arthritis found in older persons.

OSTEOARTHRITIS

Osteoarthritis is an extremely common, noninflammatory, pro-gressive disorder of movable joints, particularly weight-bearing joints, characterized by deterioration of articular cartilage and by formation of osteophytes in the subchondral areas and at the margins of the joint.[2] The functional areas most affected in older persons are the knees, hips, and the distal interphalangeal joints.

Limitations in motion may be due to acute synovitis caused by minute fragments of cartilage that enter the synovial fluid and the inability of joint surfaces to slide smoothly due to cartilage deterioration. Muscle spasms, in addition to pain, can limit motion. Osteophytes cause motion limitation because of the pain from the stretching of the periosteum as well as blocking motion by their physical presence. Muscular weakness due to disuse inhibits full motion.

RHEUMATOID ARTHRITIS

Rheumatoid arthritis is a progressive disease in which inflammation of movable joints is frequently combined with extra-articular disorders. The disease has a tendency for remissions and exacerbations. The clinical picture of someone with rheumatoid arthritis involves swelling in many joints, fatigue, slight fever, and morning stiffness. Although it affects mainly women in their 20s and 30s, another peak incidence occurs in persons over 65 years of age.

Limitations in motion result from adhesions between joint surfaces, which can be transformed into an ankylosed joint. Weakened supporting structures, such as tendons and ligaments, along with cartilage loss can cause unstable, hypermobile, or functionally limited joints. The areas most frequently affected in the older person are the hands, wrists, feet, ankles, and knees.

POLYMYALGIA RHEUMATICA

Polymyalgia rheumatica is a syndrome occurring in older individuals characterized by pain and stiffness in proximal muscle groups, with fever, malaise, weight loss, and a very rapid erythrocyte sedimentation rate. The areas most affected are the neck, back, and pelvic and shoulder girdles.

The origin of polymyalgia rheumatica is unknown. It affects both men and women, mostly those over 65 years of age. Polymyalgia rheumatica responds dramatically and completely to corticosteroid therapy; therefore, this is the best treatment and a diagnostic tool.

Since the overwhelming majority of elderly people who seek exercise programs and who have a diagnosis of arthritis have osteoarthritis, the following exercises were designed with these people in mind. Polymyalgia rheumatica requires *no* exercise intervention while the disease is in the active phase; rheumatoid arthritis will not be addressed because of its continually changing status.

EXERCISE AS AN INTERVENTION PROGRAM FOR ARTHRITIS

Why Exercise?

The ability to comb one's hair or take the wallet from one's pocket are good reasons to exercise. Exercise can maintain or increase motion; lack of exercise can contribute to muscular atrophy.

The components of muscle and joint tissue are elastic. If these structures are not stretched, they will become tighter and more limiting.[3] A common example of this is the shortening of the hip flexors that frequently occurs when a person sits for long periods. When muscle is allowed to rest in its shortened position for long periods, it slowly loses its ability to stretch to its full resting length.

Motor power is also improved by exercising, while daily movement increases or maintains strength. Nevertheless, many daily routines ignore certain muscles, which may become weaker. When muscles weaken, any activity that is different from the daily routine can be painful, difficult, and tiring. A general strengthening exercise program that uses all the muscles can prevent this from happening.

Exercise also increases the sense of well-being by increasing the body's production of chemicals that relieve pain and produce a slight euphoria.[4]

Exercise decreases tension in muscles by:

1. increasing circulation to the muscle to relieve the spasms
2. promoting maximum contraction, which causes maximum relaxation
3. increasing production of pain-relieving chemicals to break the pain-spasm cycle.[5]

Finally, exercise may actually lessen the effects of arthritis. Muscle contractions are a major shock-absorbing mechanism; therefore, if one pursues a vigorous exercise program to strengthen the muscles surrounding weight-bearing joints, they will be better protected.

When To Exercise

Exercise is best in short, frequent sessions and thus does not overtax the individual. It is much better to exercise three times a day for 15 minutes than once a day for 45 minutes. Optimal exercise times are early morning; the middle of the day; and early evening. Exercise is easier when performed one hour after the administration of oral pain-relieving medicines. Any pain relievers applied topically work best immediately, and exercises should be done immediately after they are applied.

One should not exercise when tired. Fatigue may indicate potassium depletion,[6] which is common in older persons. Potassium is needed by the muscles for contraction; the extra exertion necessary in a depleted state deprives the individual of any benefits of the exercise.

How Much To Exercise

When is an exercise program excessive? When is it insufficient? A program that causes joint pain that persists more than one hour after the end of the session should be decreased in frequency or intensity. For example, if doing ten arm circles causes shoulder pain, and the pain continues for several hours after the exercise, the arm circles should be reduced to five repetitions. If the pain persists, repetitions should be decreased to three, and if the pain still persists, decreased to one repetition. If one repetition still causes persistent pain, the exercise should be changed. Motion for a given joint can be achieved by different types of exercise, some of which are less stressful to sensitive structures. A physical therapist can design a safe, effective regimen.

While exercising, an arthritic person is likely to experience slight discomfort as well as muscle soreness after the completion of exercises. Soreness can persist for up to three days but should not be confused with the joint pain discussed earlier. Muscle soreness often indicates increasing strength. Muscle soreness, as differentiated from pain:

1. does not occur in the joint, but around it; and
2. increases as pressure is applied to the muscle belly.

Where To Exercise

Exercise can be done anywhere, but some exercise positions are better than others. For instance, back lying eliminates the gravitational forces for any sideward motions. An example of this is the increased ease with which one can bring a leg to the side when in a supine as opposed to a side-lying position. Gravity can also assist in some exercises. (For example, raising the arms straight over the head is much easier in the supine position than when sitting.)

Exercises done in water have the same advantages of back-lying exercises, plus others. Water adds resistance to motion and thus improves muscle strength, while providing general buoyancy. This can be observed by slowly moving an arm in the water and letting it float to the surface. Pulling the arm down to one's side through the water demonstrates the resistance that must be overcome to do the exercise.

Standing to exercise has the advantage of stretching the muscles that become tight while sitting. Hip flexors cannot be stretched while sitting or back lying.

Exercises can be done anywhere: on a bus, at a desk, in front of a television, or in a class. Choosing the best positions for exercise is more important than where one exercises. Exercises can be adapted to any setting. Again, the most important aspect is not where but when, how much, and how the exercises are done.

How To Exercise

The key to obtaining maximum benefit from exercise is to choose exercises that suit the person's needs. Exercises serve two major needs: to improve strength and to increase flexibility.

Flexibility exercises are done slowly; the most important part of the exercise is at the point of motion where the muscles are stretching. For example, a person might wish to improve limited wrist motion. If the person bends the wrist slightly, the point of pain and tightness is where the exercise should be done, slowly and cautiously. A slight push to increase the wrist bend performed three times a session, three sessions a day will increase wrist motion. The stretching movement should never be done quickly or for a prolonged period—it should be done slowly and held for a few seconds.

Strengthening exercises that can be done without expensive equipment are of two types: isometric, and isotonic.[7] Isometric exercises are static muscle contractions that can increase strength. Performing these exercises can create problems for older persons: (1) an increase in blood pressure and (2) an increase in intracranial pressure (due to breath holding). For these two reasons isometric exercises are not recommended without individual monitoring.

Isotonic exercises are the typical "weight-training" exercises; however, it is not necessary to perform these exercises with large weights—or any weights at all. The weight of an arm or a leg in a particular exercise may be enough to increase strength of the working muscle. The important factor in doing isotonic exercises is to do them properly. Here are some pointers:

1. Don't substitute muscles. Often one can change a position slightly and use an entirely different set of muscles for an exercise. When this happens the muscle one is trying to strengthen does not receive the benefit of the exercise.
2. Never hold the breath when exercising; this increases intra-cranial pressure and could result in a stroke.
3. Avoid increasing weights too quickly. Whenever a weight is added to an exercise, the repetition should be decreased. For example, if one were doing ten elbow bends with no weights and then progressed to five pounds, the repetitions should be cut to five initially.

4. Increase weights when the exercise is done easily at 20 repetitions.
5. Increase repetitions when the exercise is done easily at a given weight. If struggling at a low number of exercises, do not increase repetitions or weights; stay at that level.

Evaluating the Need for Exercise

As mentioned, everyone should exercise, whether for the benefit of the sense of well-being or to improve motion or strength; persons with arthritis need to exercise to alleviate stiffness, spasms, discomfort, and weakness. The particular concerns of the arthritic person as they relate to the design of an exercise program are discussed in the following paragraphs.

Stiffness

The illustrations in Figure 10–1 depict the normal motion of every joint in the body. While it is not necessary for the patient to equal these ranges, the pictures can be used as comparisons for joints that seem to be particularly tight. Comparison to the normal can provide a goal for the exercise program; the point of flexibility exercising, however, is to strive for functional motion, rather than full, normal motion. Working needlessly to achieve full range may be a waste of time. An example of this could be exercising to increase wrist flexion. Since the normal 90 degrees of wrist flexion are not needed for daily activities, a more realistic, functional goal would be 45 degrees of flexion.

Spasm and Discomfort

Spasms are uncomfortable lumps or areas of tightness in the muscles. They occur around a joint or along the muscle belly; often, they are tender to the touch. Spasms and discomforts may worsen with certain activities, such as vigorous strengthening exercises or jerky, rapid motions.[8] Therefore, if spasms or other discomforts in joints and muscles occur, one should relax and then engage in   gentle range of motion exercises.

Figure 10–1 Range of Normal Joint Motions

Shoulder	
Flexion	0–180*
Hyperextension	90–50

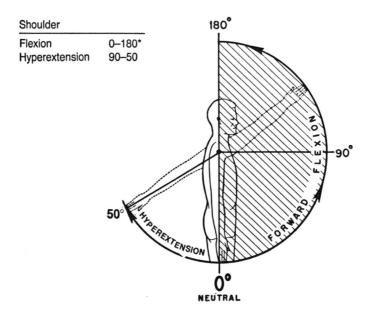

Shoulder	
Abduction	0–180
Adduction	75–0

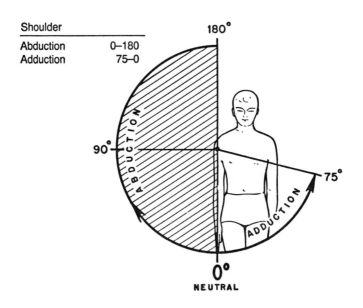

*All figures given refer to degrees of motion.

Figure 10–1 continued

Shoulder Rotation

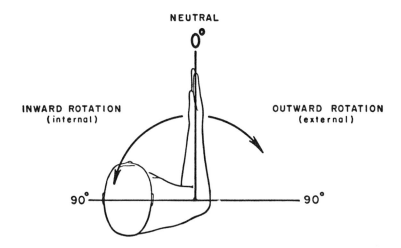

Elbow

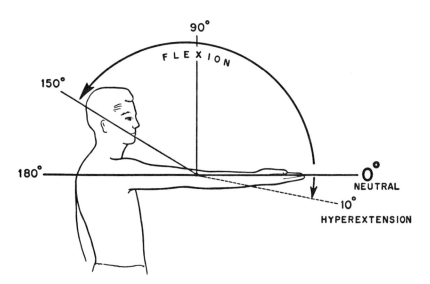

Figure 10–1 continued

Radio-Ulnar

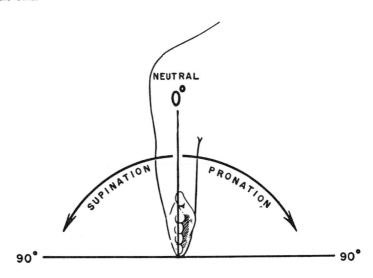

Wrist (flexion)

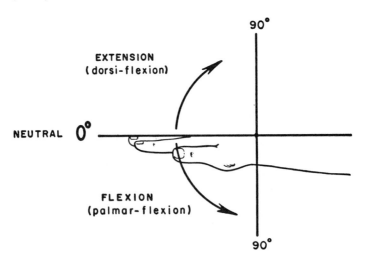

Figure 10–1 continued

Wrist

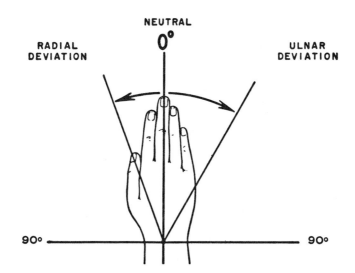

Fingers—Metacarpophalangeal Joint

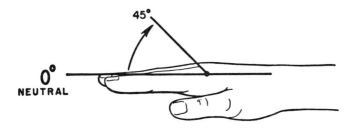

Fingers—Proximal Interphalangeal Joint

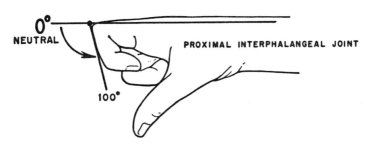

Figure 10–1 continued

Fingers—Distal Interphalangeal Joint

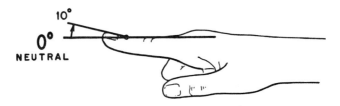

Thumb—Metacarpophalangeal

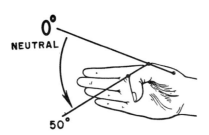

Thumb—Interphalangeal Joint

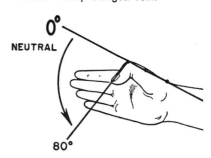

Toes—Metatarsophalangeal Joint

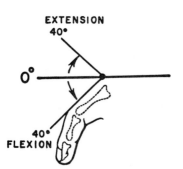

Toes—Interphalangeal Joint

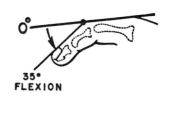

Figure 10–1 continued

Flexion (bent knee)

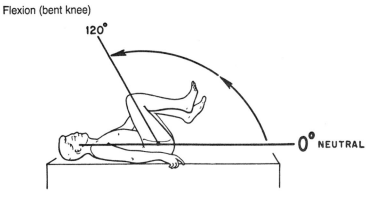

Extension

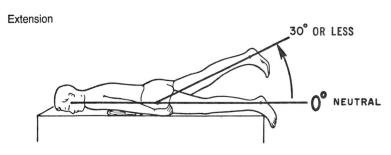

Hip

Abduction	0–45
Adduction	45–0

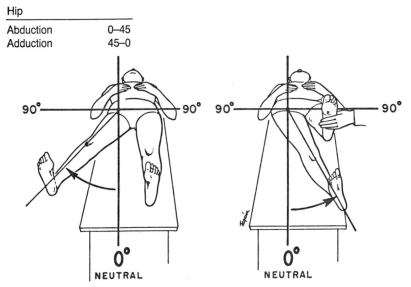

Figure 10–1 continued

Hip Rotation

External rotation	0–45
Internal rotation	0–45

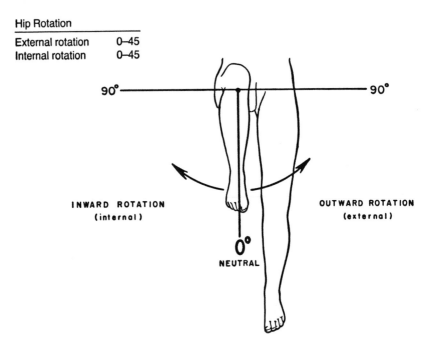

Knee

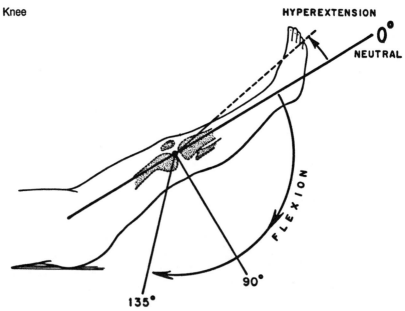

Figure 10–1 continued

Ankle

Flexion	0–20
Extension	0–50

Foot

Eversion	0–25
Inversion	0–35

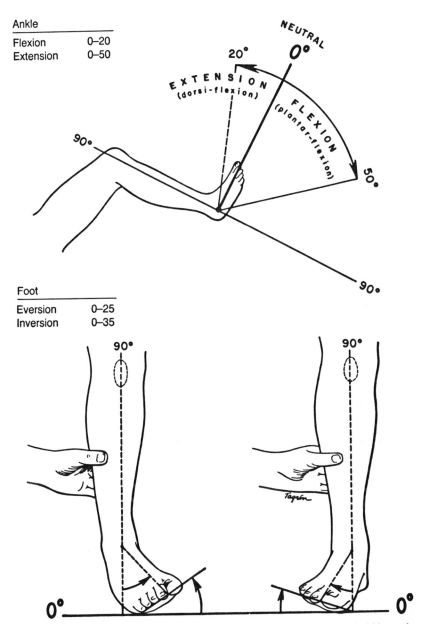

Weakness

If holding a coffee pot, walking three blocks, lifting a bag of groceries, or performing any daily activity is arduous, then weakness is a problem. Any activity that was formerly done with ease and is now difficult may be a result of weak muscles around a joint. This is true even if the initial cause of the problem was pain: a painful joint will be used less, consequently the surrounding muscles get weaker because of disuse.

To assess strength the individual should look closely at his or her daily activities. If an activity is difficult or becoming difficult to accomplish, exercises to sustain the relevant muscles should be started; if an activity is being performed with less intensity, exercises for the muscles involved in that activity should be begun. For example, if someone now walks shorter distances, exercises to increase leg strength should be performed.

Designing an Exercise Program

Arthritis exercise programs are of two major types:

- general programs that incorporate exercises for strength, range of motion, and relaxation
- specific programs designed for either strength, flexibility, or relaxation of particular body areas.

General Programs

General exercise programs should start slowly and easily with warm-up exercises, such as:

1. deep breaths, three times
2. shaking all joints
3. shrugging shoulders
4. moving parts of the body in a wave-like motion.

Warm-up exercises should be followed by   range of motion and strengthening exercises, progressing through all the joints. For example:

1. Neck motions done slowly, feeling the stretch three times (do not turn the head in a circle, which might cause dizziness)
2. Shoulder shrugs (forward and backward)
3. Wand exercises for each shoulder
4. Hands

   • Make a fist, first with the thumb in and then with the thumb out _____ times each;
   • Stretch the fingers apart, then bring them together _____ times;
   • Pull the thumb to the tip of each finger, making a circle.

5. Standing

   • Twist the trunk to the right and left.
   • Bend the body forward, backward, and to each side.
   • Holding on to a chair, lift each leg out to each side, front, and back.

6. Sitting

   • Bring each knee to the chest.
   • Bend and straighten each knee (three times).
   • Turn the heels in and out (three times).
   • Bend the feet up and down (three times).
   • Turn the feet in and out (three times).
   • Make circles with each foot (three times).
   • Perform towel curls with the toes (three times).

These exercises provide general mobility and mild strengthening for almost all joints, without causing undue stress. All the exercises can be performed in a sitting, standing, or lying position. These exercises can also be modified by increasing the repetitions and by adding weights. (See "How Much" section for details on how to do this.)

The exercise program should end with a "cool-down" session, repeating the warm-up and relaxation exercises in the reverse order. The program should start slowly and should not exceed a 30-minute duration, if three repetitions of each exercise are done.

Specialized Programs

Specializing the program to meet particular strength, mobility, or relaxation needs entails eliminating exercises that are too easy or cutting repetitions to allow inclusion of new exercises. Another alternative is to do specific exercises at a different time during the day.

An exercise program for one body part should include exercise of the joints and muscles above and below the specific part. An example of this would be to do hip and ankle exercises for a knee problem, along with knee motion and strengthening exercises.

Inner tube exercises are specific strengthening exercises that can be done with an inner tire tube or any similar stretchy object. These exercises provide gentle strengthening and mobility for the involved body part. The outstanding aspect of this technique is that it enables the patient to govern the stretch and strengthening according to the degree of pain experienced; thus, the resistance should never be too great.

Jacobson's Relaxation Exercises are highly recommended for individuals who suffer from pain, anxiety, and/or muscle spasms. The exercises increase circulation to the body parts, helping the muscles to relax to their resting length. Relaxation procedures can be performed separately from the general program or can be added to the program. Other relaxation techniques include yoga, autogenic training, visual imagery, and meditation. (More information on these techniques can be found in the popular literature.) Exhibit 10–1 is an example of Jacobson's Relaxation Exercises.

Group and Individual Programs

Designing the ideal individual program requires careful screening of the patient and careful selection of exercises to meet that patient's needs. Group exercise planning is different: a general group assessment is done and various exercise components chosen. For example, a knee pain

Exhibit 10–1 Jacobson's Progressive Relaxation Exercises

Get as comfortable as you can and relax as fully as possible.

As you do each of the exercises, tense the appropriate muscles and try to keep the rest of the body fully relaxed. You want to become as sensitive as possible to the difference between the feelings of tension and the very pleasant sensations of relaxation. Therefore, pay constant attention to the feelings in the muscles you are working with and in the body as a whole. Between exercises, relax the whole body.

1. *Right Fist:* clench it tightly; study the tension; relax; observe the contrast.
2. *Left Fist:* clench it tightly; study the tension; relax; observe the contrast.
3. *Both Fists:* clench it tightly; study the tension; relax; observe the contrast.
4. *Bend elbows and tense biceps in both arms:* relax by letting arms rest at side.
5. *Straighten arms and tense triceps in back* of arm.
6. *Face:* wrinkle forehead tightly.
7. *Frown:* crease brow.
8. *Tighten eyes:* close them hard.
9. *Jaws:* clamp them shut.
10. *Press tongue hard* against the roof of your mouth.
11. *Neck:* press head back as far as it will go; then shift forward until your chin is on your chest. Then back up until relaxed.
12. *Shoulders:* shrug (pull your head down between your shoulders).
13. *Chest:* breathe deeply; hold breath in; then exhale easily and breathe regularly and freely.
14. *Stomach:* tighten abdominal muscles, making them hard.
15. *Buttocks and thighs:* press heels into floor.
16. *Lower back:* arch the back and make it hollow.
17. *Calf muscles:* press feet down; bring toes up.

class begins with the class participants evaluating their knee, hip, and ankle motion and strength. Classes would consist of a general range of motion exercises for the hip, knee, and ankle; Jacobson's Relaxation Exercises would conclude the sessions. Participants would be expected to do each of the sets of exercises daily (or at least three times) during the week. Time spent in class would be devoted to the exercise programs and checking programs for difficulties with exercise technique and exercise progression.

Pain Relievers

Pain relievers range from aspirin to herbs to prescription drugs. The use of oral medication influences the timing of exercise, since it takes time for the medication to become digested and enter the circulatory system. Oral pain relievers generally should be taken either during or after the exercise program. If pain is being used as an indicator of the extent of safe exercising, then the medication should be taken after the exercise, so that the pain will be an accurate indicator. If, however, the participant feels so much pain that even the mildest motion is impossible during the exercise session, but not one hour after, then taking the pain reliever at least one hour prior to exercising is advantageous.

Topical Agents

Ice. Ice acts as a pain reliever and anti-inflammatory agent. After exercising, ice can be applied in a plastic bag to the painful area for 20 to 30 minutes. The area will feel cold, then burning, then painful, and finally numb. Some people have a very difficult time tolerating the first stages of ice application and cannot gain the benefits of its later stages. Those who can tolerate ice can apply it as often as five times a day.

Heat. Hot pads, bottles, and blankets provide a comfortable warmth that aids relaxation. Heat assists in bringing about pain relief because it is a counterirritant to pain and because it improves superficial circulation. Superficial heat is less effective than ice in decreasing inflammation and relieving pain. Heat is, however, much easier and more comfortable to tolerate. Heat is applied to the painful area for 20 to 30 minutes, three to four times a day.

Both heat and ice applications require protection of the skin. Older persons tend to have fragile skin and can get heat or ice burns easily. Burns can be avoided by putting extra towels under the heating or cooling element, turning heating units to low settings, and checking the skin under the heat pad or ice bag periodically. Heat should never be used on a swollen joint or muscle; ice will decrease swelling, whereas heat will increase it.

Bandages may be advantageous when used as a method of retaining superficial heat or as a pain reliever. They are relatively easy for an older person to apply but should be checked to assure enough looseness not to restrict motion or compromise the venous system. Linaments are a popular form of heat and pain reliever, especially among the elderly. Linaments act as counterirritants and may be as effective as more expensive treatments.

CONCLUSIONS

The older person with arthritis can be helped: providing education on appropriate exercise programs is a start; encouraging groups to exercise together and express ideas and concerns about arthritis is a second step. Supporting the individual to feel self-confident about controlling pain, immobility, and weakness is an attainable goal for the health professional who takes the time to analyze the special problems of the older person who suffers from arthritis.

NOTES

1. Arthritis Foundation's "Primer on the Rheumatic Diseases" no. 4, reprinted from the *Journal of the American Medical Association* 224, no. 5 (April 30, 1973).

2. Ibid.

3. R. Memmler, *The Human Body in Health and Disease* (New York: J.B. Lippincott, 1977).

4. F. Steinberg, *Cowdry's The Care of the Geriatric Patient* (St. Louis, Mo.: C.V. Mosby, 1976).

5. S. Lecht, *Therapeutic Exercise* (Baltimore, Md.: Waverly Press, 1969).

6. Memmler, *The Human Body.*

7. R. Harris, *Guide to Fitness after Fifty* (New York: Plenum Press, 1977).

8. B. Ziebell, *Wellness: An Arthritis Reality* (Toronto: Kendall Hunt Publishing Co., 1981).

Chapter 11

Food for Fitness

Leonard Biegel

No guide to fitness would be complete without first commenting on dietary habits. As with exercise, moderation and regularity are the bywords. Clients, particularly those over 65, must be reminded that poor eating habits, such as consuming too much sugar and fat, cannot be erased simply by exercise. At the same time, they must be reminded that an adequate total diet is essential for best daily bodily functioning.

Older people, particularly those who are suddenly alone and who may be on limited budgets, are apt to neglect what they know to be balanced nutrition. No amount of exercise will remedy dietary deficiencies.

NUTRITIONAL REQUIREMENTS OF OLDER ADULTS

While the nutritional requirements of the older adult are basically those of a younger person, fewer calories are needed. Foods high in proteins, minerals, and vitamins should be consumed so that the reduced food intake will still provide the needed nutrients. Decrease in physical activity, loss of sensitivity to taste and smell, dental impairment, solitary dining, and reduced income affect the eating habits of older adults.

Although the body's need for protein does not decrease with advancing age, many older people reduce their meat, fish, and poultry intake without increasing consumption of other protein-rich foods. Mineral and vitamin intake also suffers from the changes some people make in their food habits as they grow older. In addition, calcium and ascorbic acid are often deficient in the diets of older men and women. Milk and cheeses can be consumed to provide calcium; citrus fruits, raw strawberries, green peppers, and broccoli are among excellent sources of ascorbic acid.

If chewing is difficult, soft fruits and juices can be substituted for firm fruits; fish and chopped meat are tender sources of protein. Appliances such as a blender, small meat grinder, and mixer are useful for reducing foods to a chewable consistency. Meat can also be ground several times by a butcher until the fibers are finely divided, and the use of meat tenderizers can make any cut of meat tender and easy to eat. Cheese and egg dishes, finely chopped and well-cooked vegetables, puddings, soups, and custards can be included in the menu. In addition, strained foods are available that require no preparation and come in a large selection of tasty and nutritious items, although these foods are often highly salted or may contain excessive sugar. If the sense of taste has declined, the use of herbs and spices and bright garnishes can make meals more appetizing.

Those concerned about the cost of food find many ways to obtain foods high in nutrients yet relatively economical. For example, canned evaporated milk and nonfat dry milk have the same protein and calcium value as that of fresh milk and frequently can be substituted for fresh milk in cooking and baking. Large packages of nonperishable items such as sugar, flour, and rice are generally less expensive per pound than are the small packages and do not lose nutritive value if properly stored for several months. In addition, low-cost cuts of meat and fish are as high in food value as are the more expensive cuts. Thrifty buys are usually available on stew meats, pot roast, and liver.

NUTRITIONAL REQUIREMENTS OF YOUNG vs. OLD ADULTS

The generally recognized daily food requirements for a balanced diet for an older adult can be compared to the needs of younger adults, as shown in Table 11–1.

Table 11–1 Daily Food Requirements, Young and Old Adults

	Young Adult Requirement	Older Adult Requirement
Milk or milk products (in cups)	2 or more	2 or more
Meat, fish, poultry, eggs (in 3-oz. servings)	2 or more	2 or more
Green and yellow vegetables (in servings)	2	at least 1
Citrus fruits and tomatoes (in servings)	1	1 to 2
Potatoes, other fruits, and vegetables (in servings)	1	0 to 1
Bread, flour, and cereal (in servings)	3 to 4	2 to 3
Butter or margarine (in servings)	2 to 3	1 to 2

In using Table 11–1, note that:

- Individuals need not eliminate foods they like—they simply should conform to the needed quantities.
- The nutrients in one or two cups of milk can be obtained in cheeses or ice cream (one cup of milk is approximately equivalent to 1½ cups of cottage cheese or two to three large scoops of ice cream). Ice cream, however, has considerable amounts of sugar, which is contraindicated in the diabetic diet.
- One should drink the equivalent of three to five cups of fluids daily.
- Meat, fish, and poultry may be alternated with eggs or cheese, dried peas, beans, or lentils, although most vegetable protein is incomplete.
- Women should consume iron-rich foods (liver, heart, lean meats, shellfish, egg yolks, legumes, green leafy vegetables, and whole grain and enriched cereal products) as frequently as possible to help meet their high requirement for this mineral.

- Although many older people need vitamin pills, a vitamin supplement should be taken only under the advice of a physician.
- The interaction of a particular food with the elder person's medication should be discussed with the physician.
- Alcohol and tobacco are more dangerous in the advanced years. While moderate alcohol intake is permissible for most people, it should remain moderate because an older person's liver is less efficient.

PRESENTING DIETARY INFORMATION

Fitness class is a perfect setting for discussing balanced diets, and the information can be presented in interesting, often eye-opening fashion. The group leader can, for example, assign each member to research a particular aspect of nutrition once a week for presentation to the group. Consider, for example, the list of calorie reductions in Table 11–2.

Table 11–2 Reductions in Calories

Foods	Calories Saved
Instead of 1 tablespoon margarine or butter, use nonstick fry pan	100
Instead of margarine on bread, use jelly	60
Instead of a mixed alcoholic drink, have a glass of dry wine	115
Instead of cream, use milk in coffee	20
Instead of whole milk, drink skim milk	60
Instead of sour cream in recipes, use low-fat yogurt	100
Instead of filled cookies, eat plain vanilla wafers or tea cookies	60
Instead of fruit pie, eat a baked apple or a pear	300
Instead of ice cream or sherbet, eat ice milk	55
Instead of a blueberry muffin, have a slice of bread	55

Source: Courtesy of Continental Baking Company, "How To Heave out The Heavies in Your Diet," Rye, N.Y.

OBESITY AND OTHER DIETARY HEALTH RISKS

Controlling obesity is the primary work of health professionals who work with older people, for overweight is known to shorten the life span. As Dr. Nathan Shock, former director of the National Institutes of Health's Gerontology Research Center put it: "If you could suddenly have a wand and eliminate all obesity in the population, you'd be more likely to increase life span than by almost any other means."[1]

Older people, especially, should be advised against "crash" or "fad" diets. Many of these diets promise rapid weight loss but all too frequently risk extreme imbalance in the required nutrients. Furthermore, these extreme diets are difficult to maintain over a long period.

Salt, fat, and sugar are major concerns for all age levels, especially those over 65. Growing evidence supports the relationship between stroke, hypertension, and heart disease and the above-mentioned food elements. Once again, clients should be advised that moderation is the key. Fresh fruits should be eaten for dessert in lieu of cookies and cakes; poultry and fish should be alternated with red meat; salt should be avoided altogether.

CALORIC INTAKE AND EXPENDITURE

While moderation is the recurring byword, many people express interest in the duration and type of exercise needed to burn off certain types of food. This analysis, provided by the U.S. Department of Agriculture, shows the approximate number of calories it takes to perform various activities, from sedentary to strenuous:

It takes 80 to 100 calories per hour to perform sedentary activities such as reading, writing, watching TV, sewing, or typing; 110 to 160 calories per hour for light activities such as walking slowly, ironing, or doing dishes; 170 to 240 calories per hour for moderate activities such as walking moderately fast or playing table tennis; 250 to 350 calories per hour for vigorous activities such as walking fast, bowling, golfing, or gardening; and 350 or more calories per hour for strenuous activities such as swimming, tennis, running, dancing, skiing, or football.

One way of relating calories to activity level is to show how many minutes of various activities are needed to burn off a given number of food calories. For example, if one is relaxing in front of the TV set, it will take more than an hour to burn off the calories in two tablespoons of peanuts (105 calories); but if one swims or plays tennis, it will take less than 20 minutes.

Older people, in particular, should plan caloric intake according to their level of activity. If they are very active, they may need extra food for added energy. If they are sedentary, they should reduce calories. Many experts say it is wiser to increase activity rather than to reduce caloric intake drastically.

NOTE

1. Nathan Shock, personal communication.

Index

A

Adams, Gene, 5
Adipose tissue, 15
Administration, dance therapy and, 114-15
Aerobic capacity, 17, 48
Aerobic fitness, 24-25
  swimming and, 120
  walking and, 89-90, 91, 92
Agility, 19
Aging process
  inactivity and, 101-102
  body function and exercise and, 18-19
  effects of exercise on, 8-9
  MacArthur on, 38-39
Alcohol intake, 57, 154
Aldrich, Daniel G., Jr., 34
Alternate arm lifts, 80
Alternate below to knee touch
  exercise, 86
American Dance Therapy Association, 103, 104
American Health Care Corporation, 7
American Medical Association, 95
Angina, 6

Angry cat-swayback horse exercise, 80-81
Ankle circles exercise, 71
Appetite, 28
Arm chair pushups, 77
Arm exercises, 62
Arm length, 15
Arm swinging knee-benders exercise, 87
Arterial plaque, 6
Arteriosclerosis, 101-102
Arthritis
  dance therapy and, 110
  intervention program and, 131-49
  osteoarthritis, 129-30
  polymyalgia rheumatica, 130-31
  rheumatoid, 130
  swimming and, 120
The Autocrat of the Breakfast Table (Holmes), 90

B

Back lying (in water), 133
Backward body bridge exercise, 79
Balance, 18, 64

Basal metabolic rate, 16, 41, 49
Basketball, 24
Bicycling, 24
  exercise (in air), 79
  on nonmotorized stationary bicycles, 44
Blood pressure and characteristics, 41
Bodily movement, 8
Body positions, 63
Bowling, 25, 45
Brazil, Joan, 34
Breathing, 63
Byrd, J., 47

C

Calisthenics
  aerobic fitness and, 24
  caution and precaution and, 64-65
  chair-supported activities, 74-77
  evaluating, 44-45
  everyday activities and, 64
  floor activities and, 77-82
  general guidelines for, 62-63
  goals of, 61-62
  rhythmic movements in sitting
    position and, 66-74
  standing activities and, 62, 82-87
  swimming and, 120
Calories
  defining K-, 42
  expenditure of, 45, 46
  intake and expenditure and, 155-56
  older adults and, 151
  reduction in, 154
  swimming and expenditure of, 120
  walking and expenditure of, 90, 91
Canadian 5BX program, 7
Capillaries, 9
Cardiac rehabilitation, 42
Cardiorespiratory fitness, walking
  and, 92
Cardiovascular conditioning, 45
Cardiovascular system, avoiding
  sauna and, 65

Carpenter, Paul, 35
Chace, Marian, 104, 107
Chair-supported activities, 74-77
Chewing, 152
Chicago Park District, 27
Children, growth traits and, 14-16
Cholesterol, 5, 47
Cigarette smoking, 10, 56, 154,
  walking and, 92
Circle formation (dance therapy), 105
Circulation, 8, 18
Climate, 52
Clothing, 65
  walking, 96-97
Coastline Community College, 34
Comfort, Alex, 29
Confused patients, dance therapy
  and, 107, 109
Congestive heart failure, 6
Cognitively impaired, dance therapy
  and, 109
Conrad, Casey, 3-4, 27, 32
Consent letter, 55
Convalescent homes, 35
Cool-down routines, 73-74
  arthritis program and, 146
  walking, 93-95, 98
Coordination, 19
Coronary heart disease
  exercise and minimizing, 5
  mortality rate and, 10
Costs
  food, 152
  medical care, 32-33
Crawl stroke exercise, 71
Creative movement therapy. See Dance/
  movement therapy
Cureton Physical Fitness Course for
  Adult Men, 45-46
Cureton, Thomas K., 7, 8, 37-38

D

Dance, 25
Dance/movement therapy
  benefits of, 109, 112

conclusions concerning, 117
contraindications, 113
defining, 103-104
establishing program for, 114-16
goals of, 103
history of, 104
motivation and, 113-14
techniques, 105-109
Data
  dietary, 154-55
  on exercise, 1, 2
Davis, John T., 92
Degenerative illness, 110
Depression, 102
deVries, Herbert, 5, 30
Diabetes, 6
  avoiding sauna and, 43
Diet
  groups and, 51
  obesity and, 155
  presenting information concerning,
    154
  saturated fats and, 10
  vascular disease and, 6
Disabled, dance therapy and, 106,
  110-11, 114
Disoriented patients, dance therapy
  and, 107, 109
Drinkwater, Barbara, 16
Drug intake, 57

E

Edge-holding drills (swimming),
  124-25
Electrocardiogram (stress), 21
Elevated blood lipids, 6
Emergency services, 10
Emeritus Institute, 34-35
Emotional benefits of fitness, 36-39
Emotional disturbance, dance therapy
  and, 111-12
Empathic movement, dance therapy
  and, 107
Endurance, 49
  cardiopulmonary, 5

exercise and, 8
of heart and lungs, 18
machines and, 25
muscular strength and, 18
progression to, 74
rating of exercises and, 23
Entertainment, 112
Everyday activities, 64
Exercise
  aging process and, 8-9
  body function and, 18-19
  delayed reaction and, 41
  emotional benefits and, 36-39
  financial benefits and, 32-33
  guidelines for, 19-22
  improving fitness and, 7
  mix of, 58
  mortality rate and, 9-10
  most popular, 1-3
  motor power and, 131
  myths concerning, 28-30
  needs of older adults and, 4
  physiological responses of women
    to, 16-17
  research-supported advantages of,
    4-7
  self-image and, 7
  social benefits and, 33-36
  tranquilizing effect of, 5
Exercise programs
  arthritis and intervention and, 131-49
  bowling and, 45
  calisthenics, 44-45
  clarifying advantages of, 4
  conclusions concerning, 49
  convalescent homes and, 35
  dance/movement, 114-16
  designing, 57-58
  evaluation of, 7, 22-25
  first meeting of, 56
  golf and, 45-46
  groups and, 51-52
  handball and, 45
  jogging, 46-47
  lifestyle inventory and, 56-57
  nonmotorized bicycle, 44

older adult's perceptions of, 3-4
passive, 43-44
personal testimonies and, 27-28,
    30-31, 32-33, 35
physiological benefits from, 42-43
pre-exercise evaluation of
    participants in, 53-54
progression and, 20
raising of, 43-48
result analysis and, 58-59
rowing machine, 48
swimming, 48, 119-20
treadmill, 47-48
walking, 46, 91-93
Exercise and Sports Sciences Review, 16
Extension exercises (swimming),
    126-27
Eyes, exercise cautions and, 64

F

Facilities, 52
    dance therapy, 116
Family Health (Irwin), 24
Fat, 155
Fatigue, 6, 63, 132
Females. *See* Women
Financial benefits of fitness, 32-33
Fitness activities. *See* Exercise
Fitness programs. *See* Exercise
    programs
Flexibility, 19
    arthritis and exercise and, 134, 135
    swimming and, 119
Floor activities, 77-82
Flournoy, Myrna, 35
Food. *See* Calories; Diet; Nutrition
Food costs, 152
Fruit, 155

G

Goals
    calisthenics, 61-62
    chair-supported activity, 74-75

dance/movement therapy, 103
fitness program, 103
floor activity, 77
standing activity, 82-83
walking route and, 97
Golf, 25, 45-46
Gout, 6
Groups
    arthritis program and, 146-48
    dance therapy, 105, 108, 113-14,
        116
    exercising in, 51-52
    organizing, 52
Growth rate (children), 14-16

H

Handball, 45
Hands up, 66
Harris poll, exercise data and, 2
Harris, Dorothy, 14
Head and shoulder curl, 80
Heart
    avoiding sauna and disease of,
        43, 65
    exercise and aging and, 8-9
    exercise guidelines and, 21
    exercise and pounding of, 63
    growth traits and size and rate of, 16
    mortality and diseases of, 10
Heart attack, walking and, 90
Heat (as pain reliever), 148-49
Heel raiser and in-place running
    exercise, 85-86
Heel raise to drop seat exercise, 76
Height, sexual differences and, 15
High stepping, 66-68
Hip flexors (in water), 133
Hippocrates, 90
Hip twister, 80
Hocus-pokus exercise, 72
Holmes, Oliver Wendell, 90
Hrachovec, Josef P., 30
Hypertension, 6, 10, 29
    avoiding sauna and, 43
    walking and, 90

I

Ice (as pain reliever), 148
Ice skating, 24
I don't know exercise, 69
Imagery, dance therapy and, 108
Inactivity, aging and, 101-102
Income
  benefits of fitness and, 32
  exercise levels and, 3
Independence, 33
Inner tube exercise, 146
Inside leg swing, 76
Instructions, language use and, 111
Intensity (defining), 42
Interval training, 21
Iron cross exercise, 86-87
Irwin, T., 24
Isometric exercises, 28, 29
Isotonic exercises, 28, 134

J

Jacobson's relaxation exercises, 146, 147
Jogging, 44
  compared with walking, 90, 92
  exercise program evaluation and, 22-24, 46-47
Joint motions, exercise and, 136-43, 145, 146
Journal of Applied Physiology, 93
Jurew, Jane, 27-28

K

Knee to chin exercise, 77-79
Knee grabber, 69-70
Knee pull walking exercise, 94
Knee squeezers exercise, 72
Kraus, Hans, 6
Kuntzleman, Charles T., 43

L

Lap swimming, 127-28. *See also* Swimming

Leg exercises, 62
Leg-trunk proportion, 15
Lewis, Madalynne, 32-33
Life expectancy, 9, 11
Lifestyle inventory, 56-57
Limber up (stretch), 76. *See also* Warming-up exercises
Log roller exercise, 81

M

MacArthur, Douglas, 38-39
Machines, 25, 29
  rowing, 48
  treadmill, 47-48
Males. *See* Men
Marine Intertidal Ecology, 34-35
Massage, 43-44
Maybe exercise, 69
Mayer, Jean, 6
Medical care costs, 32-33
Medication
  antidepressant, 112
  arthritis and pain relieving, 148
  exercise and pain relieving, 132
  food and, 154
  muscular tension and tranquilizer, 37
Memories. *See* Reminiscing
Men
  exercise and, 8
  physical activity and, 3
  polymyalgia rheumatica and, 131
  sports and, 17
Mental achievement, 4, 37
Metabolism, 16, 41, 49
Mobility, progression to, 74
Morale, exercise and, 5
Mortality rate, 9-11
Motivation, 20
  dance/movement therapy, 113-14
Motor power, exercise and, 131
Mule kicking exercise, 81
Muscular atrophy, 131
Muscular strength and endurance, 18
Musculature, 16
Music (dance therapy), 106

Mutual touch (dance therapy), 105
Myocardial vascularization, exercise
    and improvement in, 5
Myths about exercising, 28-30

N

National Aeronautics and Space
    Administration, 30
National Audubon Society, 98
National Campers and Hikers
    Association, 98
National Center for Health Statistics
    exercise data, 1, 9
National Institute of Health's
    Gerontology Research Center, 155
Nervous system, 8
No exercise, 68
Nurses, dance therapy and, 115
Nutrition, 8
    older adults and, 151-52
    of young vs. old, 152-54

O

OASIS, 32-33
Obesity. *See* Overweight
One-arm overhead stretcher, 75-76
Organic brain syndrome, 109
Oriental bows exercise, 73
Osteoarthritis. *See* Arthritis
Overload principle, 21-22
Overweight. *See also* Weight loss
    diet and, 155
    fat reduction and, 6-7
    swimming and, 120
    walking and, 90

P

Pain
    arthritis and exercise and, 135
    arthritis and relief from, 148-49

    avoiding, 65
    exercise and low back, 6
    exercise programs and, 132-33
    medication and relief from, 132
    soreness and fatigue and, 63
    walking and, 97
Peripheral resistance, 41
Perrier Study of Fitness in America, 1
Personality deterioration, 38
Personal-social status, 5
Perspiration, 65
Physical deterioration, 38
Physical examination, 53-55, 65
Physical Fitness Research Digest, 4
Physically disabled, dance therapy
    and, 110-11, 114
Physical-motor traits, 37
Physicians, 154
    discouragement of jogging and, 47
    fitness program preparation and,
        20-21
    pre-exercise evaluation and, 53-55
    walking problems and, 97
Physiological benefits, 24, 30, 42-43,
    46
Physiological limits, 20
Physiological responses of women,
    16-17
Pollock, Michael L., 93
Pool-side standing drills (swimming),
    124
Polymyalgia rheumatica. *See* Arthritis
Posture, 64
    walking and, 97
President's Council on Physical Fitness
    and Sports, 11, 27, 89, 121
Pritikin, Nathan, 5-6
Props (dance therapy), 106-107
Psychological benefits of walking, 91
Psychological limits, 20
Psychologically disturbed nursing
    home patients, dance therapy and,
        111-12, 113
Psychosocial benefits
    dance therapy and, 117
    emotional, 36-39

financial, 32-33
social, 33-36
Pulse rates, 46, 49

Q

Quality of life, 36
"Quickie Fitness Test," 59

R

Raab, Wilhelm, 6
Rating the Exercises (Consumer Guide), 23
Reach and bend walking exercise, 94
Reach out exercise, 73-74
Reality orientation, 109
Recreational activities, 112, 114-15
Recreation departments, 11
Referral criteria, dance therapy and, 116
Relaxation procedures, 146
Reminiscing, 108-109, 110, 116, 117
Research on exercise, 4-7, 37-38, 49
Research and Forecast, Inc., 7
Respiratory adjustments, 41
    research on exercise and, 49
    walking and, 46
Retirement, 32, 36
Rheumatoid arthritis. *See* Arthritis
Rhythmic movements (sitting), 66-74
Rocking chair exercise, 81-82
Rowing machine, 48. *See also* Machines
Row, row, row your boat exercise, 70
Running. *See* Jogging

S

Salt, 155
Sandel, Susan L., 104
Saunas, 25, 29, 43, 65
Schwinn Ergo-Metric Exerciser, 44
Sculling (swimming), 126, 127
Sedentary tendencies, 8, 11, 101-102
Self-esteem, 103

Self-image, fitness and, 7
Selvin, Bill, 35
Senior Olympics, 31, 34
Sex. *See* Men; Women
Shackleford, C.B., 47
Shake it loose exercise, 74
Shock, Nathan, 155
Shoes (walking), 96
Shoulder exercises, 62
Shoulder-hip differences, 15
Shoulder rotations exercise, 70
Side leg lifts exercise, 79
Side leg lunge and stretcher exercise, 85
Side rock exercise, 69
Sierra Club, 98
Sitting exercises, arthritis program, 145-46
Sitting position exercise, 66-74
Sit-up walking exercise, 94-95
Skeletal system development, 16
Sleep, 63
Slump ups exercise, 72-73
Smith, D.P., 47
Smoking, 10, 56, 154
    walking and, 92
Social aspects of exercise
    bowling and, 25, 45
    groups and, 51
Social benefits of fitness, 33-36
Softball, 25
Sound View Specialized Care Center, 111, 115
Sports
    social aspects of, 34
    women and, 13-14
Standing activities, 62, 82-87
Standing exercises, arthritis program, 145
Standing knee grabber exercise, 83
Standing water drills, 122-24
Steam baths, 25, 65
Stretcher walking exercise, 94
Steinhaus, Arthur, 64
Strength, exercise and, 8, 134, 145, 146
Stress, 6
    fitness guidelines and, 21

Storke, 10
  dance therapy and, 106, 110
  walking and, 90
Sugar, 155
Sweatsuits, 29
Swimming, 24
  arthritis and exercise and, 133
  cautionary notes and, 120-21
  evaluation of, 48
  exercises for, 121-28
  program attributes, 119-20
Swing back stretcher exercise, 82
Swinging motion, 63, 64

T

Tail lift exercise, 70-71
Tail wag exercise, 82
Tennis, 24
Tension
  dance/movement and, 102
  exercise and, 5, 6
  exercise and muscular, 37, 132
  massage and, 43-44
Therapist
  dance therapy and, 115-16
  language use and, 111
  role of, 52
  swimming and, 121
Time factor
  arthritis and exercise and, 132, 147
  defining, 42
  for exercising, 63
Toe touches exercise, 73
Treading water, 125-26, 127
Treadmill, 47-48. *See also* Machines
Triglyceride, 5
Trunk bend and stretcher exercise, 85
Trunk twister exercise, 85

U

U.S. Masters Track and Field
  Championships, 34
U.S. Public Health Service, 11
  lifestyle inventory and, 56

V

Varicose veins, swimming and, 120
Vascular disease, 5-6
Vibration, 43
Vision, balance and, 18
Visual impairments, dance therapy
  and, 105
Vitamins, 154
Vocalization (dance therapy), 106

W

Walking, 62
  as aerobic exercise, 89-90, 92
  analysis of, 90-91
  checking form for, 95-96
  developing style of, 96-98
  evaluating, 46
  everyday activities, 64
  exercise program evaluation and,
    22-24
  muscular tension reduction and, 37
  program for, 91-93
  swimming and, 120
  vascular disease and, 6
Walking! (Davis), 92
Warm-up exercises
  dance therapy, 105, 106, 109, 110
  easy, 66-69
  essential nature of, 21
  exercise routines, 62
  importance of, 83
  swimming, 121, 122
  vigorous exercise and, 69-73
  walking, 93-95, 97
Weakness, arthritis and exercise and,
  144
Wear, Robert E., 53
Weight loss. *See also* Overweight
  exercise and, 6-7
  myth concerning exercise and, 28-29
  walking and, 91
Weight, sexual differences and, 15
Whirlpools, 25, 29

Windmill arm circles, 83
Wing stretcher exercise, 86
Wiswell, Robert, 28
Wolven, Gladys, 35
Women
  physical activity and, 3
  physiological responses to exercise
    and, 16-17

  polymyalgia rheumatica and, 131
  sports and, 13-14, 17
Women in Sports (Harris), 14
Wrist circles exercise, 71-72

Y

Yes exercise, 68

About the Editor

LEONARD BIEGEL is vice-president and director of media relations for Burson-Marsteller in Washington, D.C., a leading international public relations firm serving a broad range of clients, including a considerable number in the health field. Twice an Emmy Award winner for general interest television programming, Mr. Biegel is author of the widely acclaimed *The Best Years Catalogue: A Source Book for Older Americans*. He was a technical adviser to the 1981 White House Conference on Aging.

About the Contributors

M. NEEL BUELL, director of the Coastline (California) Community College Emeritus Institute, is a leader in community education programs for elderly persons seeking fitness training.

THOMAS K. CURETON, director of the Physical Fitness Institute and professor emeritus of the University of Illinois at Champaign-Urbana, is considered one of the leaders in physical fitness in the United States. He is a recipient of the Distinctive Service Award of the President's Council on Physical Fitness and Sports.

MARYELLEN KELLEHER, a dance/movement therapist, works with Dr. Sandel and her research team on various projects in Connecticut.

CAROLE LEWIS is a registered physical therapist in private practice in Washington, D.C. Ms. Lewis is an adjunct assistant professor at the University of Pittsburgh and an instructor at the University of Maryland in geriatric medicine.

SUSAN L. SANDEL, PhD., D.T.R., is a dance/movement therapist in private practice in New Haven, Connecticut. A former dance/movement therapist at the Yale Psychiatric Institute, she now serves as an adjunct faculty member at the University of New Haven and at Lesley College.

ROBERT E. WEAR is associate professor in the department of physical education, School of Health Studies, the University of New Hampshire.